# DRAMAS

### FOR

# CHILDREN.

(PRICE HALF-A-CROWN.)

# DRAMAS

## FOR

# CHILDREN:

CONTAINING

| | |
|---|---|
| THE LITTLE COUNTRY VISITOR, | VILLAGE WEDDING, |
| PRINCE HENRY, | DISTREST FAMILY, and |
| | CHARLES THE FIRST. |

---

BY THE AUTHOR OF THE BLIND CHILD.

---

London:

Printed by J. D. Dewick, Aldersgate-street,

FOR LACKINGTON, ALLEN, AND Co.
TEMPLE OF THE MUSES, FINSBURY-SQUARE.

1807.

# THE LITTLE COUNTRY VISITOR.

## A DRAMA.

### IN TWO PARTS.

"Accomplishments by Heaven were first design'd
"Less to adorn than to amend the mind."
MISS MORE'S PASTORAL.

## PERSONS.

MRS. MONTFORT,
MATILDA,        ⎫
HARRIOT,        ⎬ HER DAUGHTERS.
ROSETTA,        — A FARMER'S DAUGHTER.
MARIA,          — A YOUNG WOMAN UNDER MRS. MONTFORT'S CARE.

SCENE, *a Garden—Parlour.*

*Mrs. Montfort and Maria, at work.— Matilda and Harriot at a window; one dressing a doll, the other playing with a bandalore.*

MATILDA.

HARRIOT, don't you think my doll looks very pretty in this bonnet?

#### HARRIOT.

Yes; I wish you would make me such a one.

#### MATILDA.

Oh, to be sure!—No indeed!—Why don't you make yourself one?

#### HARRIOT.

But I don't know how.—Well, if you won't, Maria will; won't you Maria?

#### MARIA.

What, my dear?

#### HARRIOT.

Make my doll a bonnet, like Matilda's?

#### MARIA.

Perhaps—

#### HARRIOT.

Oh, only *perhaps*—

#### MARIA.

You know, Miss Harriot, it must depend on whether you behave properly, and

and whether your mama chuses it to be done.

#### HARRIOT.

Oh, but I will behave properly, and then mama will chuse it to be done.

#### MRS. MONTFORT.

We shall see that.

#### MATILDA.

I shall make my doll so many things this summer; we shall have so much time in the country.

#### HARRIOT.

Not so much time truly!

#### MATILDA.

But we shall!—The days will be very long, and we shall get up early.

#### HARRIOT.

Yes, but then we shall run in the garden, and plant flowers, and that will take up our time.

##### MATILDA.

How shall we plant flowers?—We don't know how, nor when to water them.

##### HARRIOT.

Oh, James will tell us.

##### MATILDA.

Well, I wish Miss Rosetta would come. I suppose she is pretty stupid!

##### HARRIOT.

Oh, and so aukward!—I dare say she hangs down her head, and won't speak, like those little girls we saw when we were in Devonshire.

##### MATILDA, (*laughing.*)

Oh dear!—How droll they used to be. They used to curtsey, just so, (*mimicking,*) and say, yes, miss; if you please, *miss!*—and they were so *ignorant* too!

##### HARRIOT.

Dear, yes!—They did not know how to

to dance, nor to draw, nor to do fine work.—What stupid children!

MATILDA.

Now you have made me think of them, I shall laugh if Miss Rosetta should be like them.—Harriot, don't make me laugh when she comes.

HARRIOT.

Don't *you* make me laugh.

MARIA.

But—Miss Harriot.

MRS. MONTFORT, (*to her.*)

Hush—let them alone—this will be a lesson for them—they think I don't hear.

MATILDA.

Mama, did you speak?

MRS. MONTFORT.

Yes, to Maria. (*A short pause.*)

MATILDA.

When will this girl come?—I dare say

she is afraid—she thinks she shall look aukward.

### HARRIOT.

I fancy she is not much mistaken!
(*They laugh.*)
(*A rap is heard at the parlour door.*)

### MRS. MONTFORT.

Pray come in.—Matilda open the door.

### MATILDA.

Oh dear mama, (*laughs.*)—Harriot, have done laughing.

(*Rosetta comes in, she curtsies modestly. Her dress and manner should be plain, but not aukward. Matilda and Harriot stare at her, and stifle a laugh.*)

### MRS. MONTFORT.

Come in, my dear. I am very glad to see you. How do your father and mother?

### ROSETTA.

Very well, thank you, ma'am; they desired their respects to you.

MRS. MONT-

MRS. MONTFORT.

I am very much obliged to them.—Matilda, come and speak to Miss Rosetta, and take her bonnet.

MATILDA, (*aside to Harriot.*)

To wait upon her indeed.

(*She advances affectedly and proudly towards Rosetta.*)

How do you do, ma'am? I am glad to see you.—Give me leave to take your cloak.

ROSETTA.

Thank you, ma'am; pray don't trouble yourself.

(*Matilda takes away her cloak, &c. laughing aside at Harriot.—Rosetta sees them, blushes, and looks uneasy.*)

MRS. MONTFORT.

It is a fine day, Miss Rosetta.—The country begins to look very pleasant.

ROSETTA.

Yes, ma'am.

MRS. MONTFORT.

What says your father to the present appearance of the corn?

ROSETTA.

He thinks it promises very fair, ma'am.

MRS. MONTFORT, (*to Matilda.*)

Why don't you go and talk to Miss Rosetta.—I am ashamed of you.

MATILDA, (*in a low voice.*)

Dear mama, what should I say to her?

MRS. MONTFORT.

Fye, silly child!—Maria come with me, I am going to dress; and by the time I return, I hope young people you will be better acquainted. Matilda, do all you can to amuse Miss Rosetta. Harriot, be sure you behave properly.

(*Mrs. Montfort, Maria go out.*)
(*A long pause, during which all the children look confused.*)

HARRIOT.

HARRIOT, (*to Matilda.*)
Why don't you speak?

MATILDA, (*aloud.*)
Be quiet, Harriot, you are the most provoking child!

HARRIOT.
Child!—to be sure!

MATILDA.
What, you think yourself a woman, I suppose, at nine years old!

HARRIOT.
Why not, as well as you at ten?

MATILDA.
Such nonsense!—Miss Rosetta, will you like to look at my books?

ROSETTA.
If you please, ma'am.
(*Matilda takes down several books.*)

HARRIOT, (*shewing Rosetta the bandalore.*)
Is not this a very pretty thing?

###### ROSETTA.
Yes, ma'am.

###### HARRIOT.
Will you play with it?

###### ROSETTA.
I don't know how.

###### HARRIOT, *(shewing her.)*
There you must let it fall, and then jerk the string a little—you see it winds up; there, you must keep it up.

###### ROSETTA, *(trying.)*
Is that right?

###### HARRIOT.
Yes, very right; you will soon do it. Oh, but you must not jerk it so much.

###### ROSETTA.
What do you call it, pray?

###### HARRIOT.
A bandalore; some call them, Prince of Wales's toys.

###### ROSETTA.

Little Country Visitor.  Page 10.

Laura's Visit to the Young Montforts.

ROSETTA.

Why?

MATILDA.

Oh, don't you know?—They are all the fashion. The Prince of Wales brought them in.

ROSETTA.

They are pretty, but there is no great ingenuity in playing with them, I think.

MATILDA.

Oh no, it is all a knack.

ROSETTA.

I like better a plaything which requires more skill, or else is an exercise.

MATILDA.

So do I.

ROSETTA.

But you said, ma'am, you would shew me your books.

#### MATILDA.

So I will—(*To Harriot.*)—She speaks prettily.

#### HARRIOT.

Yes, she does not seem stupid.

#### ROSETTA, (*looking at the books.*)

Oh, here is the Friend of Youth, and the Tales of the Castle.

#### MATILDA.

Yes, can you read them in French?

#### ROSETTA.

No, ma'am.

#### MATILDA.

Oh, they are charming in French.

#### ROSETTA.

I dare say they are.

#### MATILDA.

Should you not like to learn French?

#### ROSETTA.

Yes, but my father says it is not proper for me.

#### MATILDA.

### MATILDA.
Do you learn to dance?

### ROSETTA.
No, ma'am.

### MATILDA.
Dear, not to dance!—oh, that is beſt of all; I love dancing. Harriot, let us dance the Devonſhire minuet. Shall you like to ſee us?

### ROSETTA.
If you pleaſe.
*(They dance—Matilda ſings the tune.)*

### MATILDA.
Now the Scotch ſteps, Harriot.
*(They dance again—Matilda very well.)*

### MATILDA.
Oh! I am out of breath—I love the Scotch reels, and they are very faſhionable now.

### ROSETTA.
It is very pretty indeed, and you dance vaſtly well.

### MATILDA.

MATILDA.
Oh no, you flatter me!

ROSETTA.
No indeed—I hope you have not so bad an opinion of me.—Perhaps, indeed, I am no judge.

MATILDA.
Oh yes, I dare say you are.

HARRIOT.
Yes, because she admires your dancing!

MATILDA.
Harriot, you are very impertinent.

ROSETTA.
Oh, Miss Harriot only jests.

HARRIOT.
Not I, indeed!

MATILDA.
Very well, miss, I shall tell mama.

HARRIOT.
As you like it.

ROSETTA.

### ROSETTA.
But, Miſs Matilda, here is another book, which ſeems very pretty. Is it pretty?

### MATILDA.
Which do you mean?

### ROSETTA.
Mrs. Barbauld's Hymns.

### MATILDA.
Oh, that is a child's book, and ſo grave!

### HARRIOT.
A child's book!—why mama is very fond of it, and ſays it is beautiful.

### ROSETTA.
I ſhould like to read it.

### MATILDA.
Oh, I'll lend it to you.

### ROSETTA.
I ſhall be extremely obliged to you.

### MATILDA.
Oh, you'll be very welcome.—Pray do you learn to ſing?

### ROSETTA.

###### ROSETTA.

No indeed.

###### MATILDA.

Your education seems to be very confined.

###### ROSETTA.

You know I am only a farmer's daughter.

###### MATILDA.

There is something in that to be sure. I suppose, if you learn how to make butter, and sell eggs, your father is satisfied?

###### ROSETTA.

Not entirely with that.

###### MATILDA.

I learn to sing.—Do you love singing?

###### ROSETTA.

Yes, indeed, very much.

###### HARRIOT.

Matilda wants to be asked to sing.

MATILDA.

Harriot, you are excessively impertinent.

ROSETTA.

I am sure I shall be happy to hear you.

MATILDA.

Oh, indeed, I am very hoarse.

ROSETTA.

Pray then don't trouble yourself.

MATILDA.

Nay, to oblige you, I'll try.
(*She sings.*)

ROSETTA.

Very pretty, indeed.—That is a charming song.

MATILDA.

I declare, Miss Rosetta, you have a great deal of taste.

ROSETTA.

Have I?

MATILDA.

MATILDA, (*aside to Harriot.*)
How simple she is!

HARRIOT.
I like her very well.

MATILDA, (*aloud.*)
But if you neither dance nor sing, how do you contrive to fill up your time?

ROSETTA.
Oh, I have a great deal to do.

MATILDA, (*to Harriot.*)
I suppose she milks the cows!

ROSETTA.
No, Miss Matilda, I don't.

MATILDA, (*embarrass'd.*)
What!

ROSETTA.
You thought I did not hear you!

MATILDA, (*very much confused.*)
I beg your pardon.

ROSETTA.

###### ROSETTA.

Oh, I am not angry; if you are amufed, that is enough.

###### MATILDA.

You are extremely good—I did not mean—

###### ROSETTA.

You did not mean to offend me. I know that one ought not to be angry at a jeft.

###### MATILDA.

You are very obliging.

###### HARRIOT.

Now, Matilda, you are fairly caught; it ferves you right.

###### MATILDA.

Harriot, I did not afk you to interfere.

Mrs. Montfort *and* Maria *come in.*

###### MRS. MONTFORT.

So, young people!—Heyday, Matilda, what's

what's the matter?—You look confused.—What have you been doing?

MATILDA.

Nothing, mama.

MRS. MONTFORT.

Oh, don't tell me that, I know better.—What was it?

HARRIOT.

Mama, she spoke impertinently of Miss Rosetta.

MRS. MONTFORT.

Harriot, that is a great fault, but it is a greater to be so eager to accuse your sister. My children, learn, that if you fail to conceal and excuse the errors of each other, the world will still more eagerly publish, and still more bitterly condemn them.—Where, alas! shall those who are faulty, look for pity and forgiveness, if not to those kindred bosoms who, knowing their failings, know also their virtues.—If we ourselves point the arrows of satire and reproach,

reproach, at our sisters and our friends, who will hold before them the shield of allowance and pardon!—This is not, however, intended to excuse you, Matilda. I am sorry, indeed, to hear you have behaved ill.

### ROSETTA.

Dear ma'am, indeed it was a mere jest, a trifle, I assure you.

### MRS. MONTFORT.

Very well, my dear, if you are satisfied.

### ROSETTA.

Yes, indeed, ma'am.

### MATILDA, (*eagerly.*)

It is more than I deserve.—Mama, I was very much to blame.—I ask your pardon, Rosetta.

### ROSETTA.

Indeed, Miss Matilda, I am not offended. I am sorry to have caused you any uneasiness.

### MRS. MONT-

MRS. MONTFORT.

You are a very good girl. I hope both your companions will profit by your example.—Let us go to dinner.

(*They go out.*)

END OF THE FIRST PART.

PART

## PART THE SECOND.

#### SCENE, *a Garden.*

*Matilda, Harriot, and Rosetta, enter from the house.*

##### MATILDA.

YOU will like our garden, I think, Miss Rosetta; it is very pleasant, and you cannot imagine how we enjoy it, after being so long in London.

##### ROSETTA.

I imagine you are very much confined there.

##### MATILDA.

Yes, indeed.—You know we live in Berkeley-square; every morning, before breakfast, we walk with our governess, who is still in town, and Maria, up and down the square for an hour.

##### ROSETTA.

###### ROSETTA.

The square—but is it like a garden?

###### MATILDA.

Oh no, there are houses on every side, and where we walk is only a pavement; so it is merely for exercise, and tiresome enough I can tell you.

###### HARRIOT.

Oh, but you know sometimes we go to the Park.

###### MATILDA.

Oh, the Park—yes, that is very fine to be sure.—There we have a long dusty walk, with trees on each side, and full of people.

###### ROSETTA.

What! no grass walks?—nor flowers?

###### MATILDA.

Flowers!—Oh no, you might look for seven years without finding one.—And on the grass we must not walk.

###### ROSETTA.

### LITTLE COUNTRY VISITOR. 25

ROSETTA.

Oh dear, how sad!—I should hate that.

MATILDA.

Oh yes, it is frightful indeed.—Sometimes we went to Kensington-gardens, which are charming, but not often.—Well, now we are in the country, we shall walk a great deal.

ROSETTA.

We have charming walks.—If Mrs. Montfort will give me leave, I will shew them to you.

MATILDA.

Oh, thank you, we shall like that vastly.

HARRIOT.

Perhaps too you know how to plant flowers, and manage them.

ROSETTA.

I have a large piece of garden, which I keep in order.

MATILDA.

What, all yourself?

###### ROSETTA.

No, the man digs it, and puts it in order; I sow the seeds, water them, tie up the flowers when they are blown, and do all that is not very fatiguing.

###### MATILDA.

How very agreeable!—What flowers have you?

###### ROSETTA.

Honeysuckles, roses, carnations, stocks, and a great variety of others, and also a large bed of thyme for my bees.

###### MATILDA.

Your bees!—Have you bees also?

###### ROSETTA.

Oh, yes, three hives.

###### MATILDA.

Oh, charming!—You are not afraid of them?

###### ROSETTA.

Dear no!—I never disturb them, and they do not hurt me.

###### MATILDA.

### MATILDA.

Are they troublesome to keep?

### ROSETTA.

Not at all. I have only to give them a little honey in the winter, to observe when they are going to swarm, and to provide a hive.

### MATILDA.

To *swarm*—what is that?

### ROSETTA.

When the hive becomes too full, a great number of young bees go out of it, to find another place, where they may make their comb, and put the honey.

### MATILDA.

Where do they get the honey?

### ROSETTA.

From the flowers. They suck it out with a sort of trunk; in passing through their bags it becomes honey. They also roll themselves in the yellow dust of flowers, which makes the wax.

##### MATILDA.

That is very curious!—You know all that!—We do not know any thing of the matter.

##### ROSETTA.

Oh, it is soon learned.

##### MATILDA.

I should like to keep bees.

##### HARRIOT.

Perhaps, mama, will let us.

##### MATILDA.

But we do not know how to manage them.

##### ROSETTA.

I will shew you, with all my heart, if you please.

##### MATILDA.

Oh, thank you, thank you; how good you are!

##### HARRIOT.

And to plant flowers also?

##### ROSETTA.

ROSETTA.

Yes, surely.

MATILDA.

Oh, delightful!—Rosetta, what flower is this?

ROSETTA.

A larkspur—Here is another, of a different colour.—They are very various in colour, and some are double.—They are annuals.

MATILDA.

What do you mean by annuals?

ROSETTA.

They last but one year—the seed must be saved, and sowed again. Most of our common flowers are annuals.

MATILDA.

Oh, but you forget roses, honeysuckles, lilacs, and jasmine?

ROSETTA.

Those are called flowering shrubs.

##### MATILDA.

How much you know!—We know nothing of all this!

##### ROSETTA.

Oh, there is nothing more eafy, when one lives in the country.

##### MATILDA.

But you have been taught all this?

##### ROSETTA.

Not at all; I need only obferve.—I do not need telling.

##### MATILDA.

And we know nothing, but what we are taught.—And yet we fancy ourfelves very wife!—No wonder your time is employed!—What elfe do you do?

##### ROSETTA.

I work a great deal.—I read whenever I can: I make cakes, and paftry: I help to gather the fruit in feafon, and to cull flowers and herbs for diftilling: I

manage

manage the poultry-yard, and overlook the dairy.

###### MATILDA.

Oh, how clever you are!—I wish I could do so.

###### ROSETTA.

There is nothing clever in that; I only do my duty.—You are differently situated, you have no need of these things.

###### MATILDA.

For all that, they are more useful.— But if we did what mama wishes us, that would be enough.

###### ROSETTA.

To be sure it is.—You do, I dare say.

###### HARRIOT.

No, truly.

###### MATILDA.

No.—Mama wishes us to read more; not to be conceited; to spend less time idly; to talk less ourselves, and attend more to other people.—Not to be impertinent; and, above all, not to quarrel.

###### ROSETTA.

No doubt, you obey such reasonable, and kind commands.

###### MATILDA.

Yes—when we remember!—But to-day—I see now how foolishly I have behaved!—How ignorant, I fancied you were, because you could not dance and sing!—How I chattered to you, without attending to what you said!—Then I was very impertinent to you, and quarrelled with Harriot.

###### ROSETTA.

But, dear Miss Matilda, how I love you for owning your faults!—You will soon mend them.

###### MATILDA.

Ah!—I fear not!

###### ROSETTA.

Yes, since you know them so well!

###### MATILDA.

You allow, then, I have faults; I love you

you for that: every body else, except Mama, my Governess, and Maria, flatter me.

ROSETTA.

To flatter!—Oh, how vile!

MATILDA.

Do they not flatter you?

ROSETTA.

No, surely; I should despise any one who did.—What! make us more faulty, by pretending to think us perfect?—Is it not vile?—Such people must either wish us to be blameable out of ill-nature, that they may ridicule us, or mean to make some advantage of our faults.

MATILDA.

I believe you are right; I shall be more cautious in future.—Rosetta promise to tell me when I am wrong.

ROSETTA.

Ah! have you not a mother, much more capable than I am of telling you?

MATILDA.

Yes; but I behave better when mama sees me.

ROSETTA.

And why?

MATILDA.

Because I know she will love me better.

ROSETTA.

What then does she wish you to *seem* good, or really to be so?

MATILDA.

Oh, really to be so, without doubt.

ROSETTA.

Then you do not answer her wishes, if you are less good when she does not see you, than when she does.

MATILDA.

Very true indeed!—Oh, you shall see I will be very good henceforward.—We shall have you with us often, I hope.

ROSETTA.

ROSETTA.

Certainly; I shall be happy, if Mrs. Montfort pleases.

MATILDA.

Oh, I am sure she will like it.—Here comes mama.—I shall ask her.—Harriot, you will like it too; shall you not?

HARRIOT.

Oh yes, indeed.

*Enter* Mrs. Montfort *and* Maria.

MATILDA, (*running to her.*)

Mama! mama!

MRS. MONTFORT.

Well!—What say you?

MATILDA.

Mama, will you not like Miss Rosetta to come and see us often?

MRS. MONTFORT.

Yes, certainly, as often as she can make it convenient to come to you.—At all hours,

hours, my dear Rosetta, if the children are taking their lessons, they shall not disturb themselves; you will not perhaps be sorry to be of the party.

#### ROSETTA.

Thank you, ma'am, you are very kind indeed.

#### MRS. MONTFORT.

I see, Matilda, by this request, that at last you understand the merit of your companion.

#### MATILDA.

Oh yes, indeed, mama!—She knows so much; she understands flowers, and how to keep bees, and to make cakes, and many other things.

#### MRS. MONTFORT.

Yes—and that is not all.—She helps her mother to instruct her sisters, in working, reading, and writing.—Besides the assistance she gives in household affairs, she works excellently well at her needle. She

She is fond of reading, and has greatly improved by it.—I beg your pardon, Rosetta, for commending you to your face, but I wish to give my children a lesson, who fancied this morning, because you had not the same advantages with themselves, you must be ignorant and aukward. They now see you are neither; and they begin to know how much more valuable and useful are your employments than theirs.

###### ROSETTA.

Indeed, ma'am, the young ladies were not mistaken; I am *very* ignorant.

###### MRS. MONTFORT.

You are very modest; which will, I hope, be another lesson to them.—Beside, Matilda, Miss Rosetta is not deficient in those lighter accomplishments which you admire so much.—She has taught herself to design landscapes, and to paint flowers, charmingly well, and she also sings very agreeably.

###### MATILDA.

MATILDA.

What! Rosetta, can you sing?

ROSETTA.

But—very little indeed.

MATILDA.

You did not say so this morning.

ROSETTA.

You only asked me, if I had *learn'd*; and, I said, I had not; which is true.

MATILDA.

Mama, I am quite convinced of what you have so often told me, that by chattering so much, attending so much to myself, and so little to other people, I lose a great deal of pleasure and instruction.

MRS. MONTFORT.

Yes.—If you had not chosen to display what you fancied your superiority, in dancing and singing, to Miss Rosetta, you would earlier have learnt her merit, and the power she has of teaching you many useful and agreeable things.—You

would

would have saved yourself the pain of being impertinent to her, and me the mortification of seeing you rude, saucy, and conceited.

MATILDA.

Mama—

MRS. MONTFORT.

Indeed, you were all these!—But, hence forward, Matilda, I hope you will reflect, that the light frivolous accomplishments you have boasted of so much are in reality of no essential import, since they neither make us more wise, more humble, or more pleasing in our behaviour.

HARRIOT.

But, mama, do you not then wish us to learn singing and dancing?

MRS. MONTFORT.

Certainly.—It is a duty incumbent on you to learn them, because I wish it, and because they are ornamental parts of education, suited to the place you are to fill

fill in life.—But I would not have you fancy they make you at all superior to those whose situation excludes them from such information.—You will do very wrong not to learn them, but you have no merit in possessing them, as every other person would do the same, if they had the same opportunity.—And I would have you always consider, that one precept which teaches you to improve your behaviour, or regulate your temper, is of more value than the finest singing, or most graceful dancing.

MATILDA.

I am sure you are right, mama.

MRS. MONTFORT.

Even superior acquirements ought not to render you proud or conceited.—If you read more, or write better, than other children of your age; if you know better how to behave, or have better qualities, you ought to reflect, that all have not equal advantages with yourself.—Every child

child has not a father, who can or will be at the expence of having her well instructed.

MATILDA.

Ah, mama, nor has every child a mother who takes such pains in teaching her!

MRS. MONTFORT.

That is true.—Learn then to make allowances for difference of natural capacity, which we have no merit in possessing, as we did not give it to ourselves; and for difference of education, which depends on those about us.—When these allowances are made, we shall seldom, if ever, find any thing to ridicule or despise; pity, and a wish to amend, will be our only sentiments.—And when we consider how many opportunities we have ourselves lost, how much more we might have learned than we have learned, we may easily allow for those who have even lost more time than ourselves.

MATILDA.

#### MATILDA.

Ah, mama, I feel how much you are in the right; and I promise you henceforth to be more attentive, and less presuming.

#### HARRIOT.

And I also, indeed, mama.

#### ROSETTA.

Ah, madam, let me too thank you for these valuable instructions; which, I hope, will be also profitable to me.

#### MRS. MONTFORT.

You are a very good girl, my dear Rosetta.—I hope you will come hither often, and that the connection will be mutually useful.—Let us go in; it is tea-time.

*(They go in.)*

*Scene closes.*

# PRINCE HENRY.

## A DRAMA.

### IN ONE PART.

"———Who conquers his own Spirit,
"He is the only Conqueror!———"
                    DAVID AND GOLIATH.

## PERSONS.

HENRY THE IVth,
PRINCE HENRY, (afterwards HENRY the Vth.)
LORD CHIEF JUSTICE,
EARL OF WESTMORLAND,
PRISONER, — One of the PRINCE's dissolute Companions.

LORD CHIEF JUSTICE. EARL OF WESTMORLAND.

LORD CHIEF JUSTICE.

THIS wild action, in which I am told the Prince is concerned, will probably cause me some uneasiness.

EARL

### EARL OF WESTMORLAND.

The Prince indeed is so unrestrained, not to say licentious, in his manners, and so urged on by his rude companions, that he is, I fear, even capable of insulting your high office; and, I am told, he means to support by his presence the criminal who is to be tried this morning.

### LORD CHIEF JUSTICE.

I fear so—but it will avail him nothing; it is my duty not to be awed by the greatest, or to overlook the meanest.— With justice there ought to be no respect of persons; and I am resolved, in my administration of it, there shall be none.

### EARL OF WESTMORLAND.

The resolution does you honour; and I am sure you will strictly keep it.

### LORD CHIEF JUSTICE.

I see the Prince coming hither, with the culprit, and his guards.—I would not, at present, wish to meet him.—Let us retire.

*Enter* PRINCE HENRY.—*The Prisoner, with Guards, and others.*

PRINCE,\*

(*Bowing to the Lord Chief Justice, as he goes off, with an air of mockery.*)

Your Lordship's most obedient.—Farewell, my very good Lord.—What, not a word!—Seest thou Will that reverend nobleman?—Dost thou not tremble?—Dost thou not feel a certain fear creeping upon thee, at the presence of thy judge?

PRISONER.

Not I, my Lord!—Your Highness's good presence gives me more courage than fifty Chief Justices could take away!

\* The Prince's wild manner of talking in this scene is not inconsistent with his behaviour afterwards, as he is represented by historians, gay and unthinking to excess, except on great occasions.

PRINCE.

PRINCE.

Say'ſt thou ſo, my lad; why then defiance to the Chief Juſtice be our motto.

PRISONER.

Mend it, my Lord—let it be defiance to all juſtices.

PRINCE.

With all my heart.—Oh, it rejoices me, to ſee the fellows bluſter a little!—at ſome poor thief, like thyſelf!

PRISONER.

Thank you, my Lord.

PRINCE.

Why, let us not flatter each other!— But is it not ridiculous?—" You fellow," ſay they, " how dared you to frighten this man?—Don't you know, ſirrah, you will be hanged ſome of theſe days." And then do I ſtep in, crying, " Your Worſhip ſays true!—Marry, your Worſhip is a wiſe man!"—Then he ſmiles, and ſimpers,
" with

with "Oh Lard, your Grace!"—And so relaxes his authority, till the poor thief escapes his Worship, who cries, " At your Grace's request.—Your Grace might command me in a greater matter!"

#### PRISONER.

Not one of them, my Lord, but believes he shall be Lord Chief Justice, when your father dies.

#### PRINCE.

Ha, ha, ha!—I cannot but laugh!—The fools; I know them; so do they not me!

#### OFFICER.

My Lord, I beg your Grace's pardon; the Court sits, and this gentleman is required to attend.

#### PRINCE.

We follow you.—Come along, Will; courage lad, we will manage the Chief Justice. *(They go out.)*

SCENE

SCENE, *the Court.*

*Lord Chief Justice on the Bench.—Earl of Westmorland.—Attendants.—Prisoner at the Bar.—The Prince by him.—Officers, and Guards, &c.*

LORD CHIEF JUSTICE.

Being thus accused, and witnesses having proved the accusation, it remains for you to clear yourself by other witnesses, who may, if it be possible, discredit the evidence already heard.

PRINCE.

My Lord, I am evidence for the prisoner.

LORD CHIEF JUSTICE.

Was your Grace present at the transaction?

PRINCE.

That matters not; suppose I can prove my friend was not there?

LORD CHIEF JUSTICE.

One witneſs, my Lord, cannot do that.

PRINCE.

What, my Lord, would you dare to diſbelieve what I ſhould aſſert?

LORD CHIEF JUSTICE.

Your Grace cannot alter the law; nor can one witneſs alone diſcredit ſo many. Your Grace may be heard, pledging your honour for the truth of what you ſay, and the Court will then judge.

PRINCE.

~~Good God!~~—What unparalleled inſolence!—*When* I have pledged my honour, the Court will judge!—Will any man here *dare* to queſtion what I ſhall ſay on ſuch a pledge?

LORD CHIEF JUSTICE.

I hope no one could.—But, my Lord, if your Grace ſtands as evidence, you muſt be heard as other evidences are.

PRINCE.

My Lord, I demand the release of the prisoner, and promise to make up matters between him and his adversary.

LORD CHIEF JUSTICE.

Your Grace must excuse me.—The prisoner cannot be released.

PRINCE.

He shall be released.

LORD CHIEF JUSTICE.

No, indeed, my Lord.

PRINCE.

We will try that.

LORD CHIEF JUSTICE.

No force shall take him from the hands of justice.

PRINCE.

Unparalleled presumption!—Do you know me?—Who am I?

LORD CHIEF JUSTICE.

I begin to hope I was mistaken: but I took you for the Prince of Wales.

PRINCE,

PRINCE, (*striking the Chief Justice, with great passion.*)
Who am I *now*?

LORD CHIEF JUSTICE, (*with dignity.*)
A ruffian—a madman, who dares insult the King, in my person.—Officers, take into custody this person, who presumes to affront me in my office.

EARL OF WESTMORLAND.
Heav'ns!—How will this end.

LORD CHIEF JUSTICE.
Do you hesitate.—Take him instantly. Convey him to prison, and let him be guarded strictly.—(*A confused murmur is heard.*)—What is that murmur?—If any person shews the least tendency to disturb the Court, take him away instantly.

OFFICERS, (*approaching the Prince.*)
Your Grace will forgive us.—Please to surrender your sword.
(*The Prince, who has stood musing, takes off his sword, and gives it to the Officers.*)

#### PRINCE.

Keep it safely.

#### OFFICER.

We shall, my Lord.

*(The Prince bows to the Court, with graceful submission, and goes out with the Officers.)*

#### EARL OF WESTMORLAND.

Heavens!—If I had not seen this, I could not have believed it.

#### LORD CHIEF JUSTICE.

Break up the Court, and guard the culprit; we shall consider of his sentence. *(They go out in order.—Prisoner guarded.)*

## SCENE changes.

*Enter the* KING, *and* EARL OF WESTMORLAND.

#### KING.

He yielded then?

#### WESTMORLAND.

Yes, my Liege, with such meek and graceful

graceful submission, he captivated all who saw him.

#### KING.

Oh! how happy am I, in having a judge who has courage enough to execute justice, even on my own son; and a son who knows so well how to submit himself to justice.

#### WESTMORLAND.

Indeed, Sire, I trembled, first at the bold action of the Prince; and again, at the proper, but alarming, resolution of the Lord Chief Justice.—I feared the Prince's companions would immediately rise to his assistance, and a riot would ensue, which, from the rank of the parties, must have proved dangerous; but his Highness, as if he had also feared this, retired with chearful obedience, and even with a submissive bow.

#### KING.

The Lord Chief Justice has pleased me well, and I shall make a point of reconciling my son to a man so worthy.

#### WESTMORLAND.

I should fear, my Liege, that might be difficult.

#### KING.

I hope it will not prove so.—I have already requested the Justice to release the Prince, and ordered Henry to come hither.—See, he is here.

#### WESTMORLAND.

Then, Sire, I will withdraw.

#### KING.

If you please, my Lord.

(*Westmorland goes out.*)

*Enter* PRINCE HENRY.

#### KING.

Harry, come hither.

#### PRINCE.

My Liege.

#### KING.

Harry, we hear of you numerous complaints.—You are indeed to blame; you lose, and others forget, the dignity of of your station, in midnight brawls, and insolent excesses.

PRINCE.

My Lord, I!

KING.

Well, well, this is not the present subject.—I sent for you to praise, not blame you.

PRINCE.

I am happy, Sir, to hear it.

KING.

Explain to me, Harry, whence it arises, that, in all your gay and thoughtless riots, you so well understood the just moment of submission?

PRINCE.

Your Grace means in the late affair with the Lord Chief Justice.

KING.

I do.

PRINCE.

My Liege, I am, as your Grace knows,

wild, thoughtless, and extravagant.—
Swayed by the ardent spirit of youth,
perhaps sometimes by motives less unworthy, I follow whither fancy leads.—
I put no restraint on myself.—I amuse
my mind by *follies*, if you please, but
harmless follies.

KING.

Harmless!

PRINCE.

Except as they respect myself.—I know,
my Liege, *that* is no excuse.—I know I
have not a right even to injure myself.—
But, my Lord, time will shew, perhaps—
Oh! misjudge me not!—Pardon me, I
am wandering.

KING.

Recover yourself, and proceed.

PRINCE.

Thoughtless as I am, then, Sire, believe me incapable of any action which
can affect your peace, or that of your
servants.

servants.—Hurried away by the tumult of paſſion, and by ſomething in his manner, which in that moment of heat I thought inſolent, I with violence, for which I bluſh, ſtruck one of your Grace's Judges, in the execution of his ſacred office.—My heart inſtantly reproached me.—The blow appeared to others, as aimed at all order—at the laws—at you. I know, my Lord, that once to take off the reſpect due to magiſtracy, is to give up the common people to riot, and to villainy.—Teach them to deſpiſe the Judge upon the Bench, and you teach them to deſpiſe the King, to deſpiſe the laws which he has made, and to own no government but that of their mad paſſions. Having myſelf ſet this dangerous example, it remained with me, by my deportment, to confirm or overthrow it.—The Chief Juſtice acted like a man; he took his reſolution, and ſupported it with dignity. I took mine, and yielded with unconditional submission: repairing thus, as far as possible, the error of a moment, which might have been followed by terrible consequences, had I been less happily able to check the pride and passion of my heart.

**KING.**

Oh, justly spoken!—With what joy, my Harry, do I see that noble heart unveiled; with what delight contemplate the difficult conquest of yourself—far, far superior in my eyes to the most brilliant victories of those the world calls heroes! far brighter and more glorious than a vanquished world!

**PRINCE.**

My King, and father!

**KING.**

Ah, Harry, I have, like others, hitherto mistook you: but I look forward now with hope, nay certainty, of glory to you, and happiness to my people, when Heaven shall place you over them!

PRINCE.

Long, long be that day delayed!

KING.

I believe you wish it; but wishes cannot check the hand of death.—Oh, my son, may those who now, and in future ages, hear of this noble action, be impelled to imitate its beauty.—May all, from the Prince to the Peasant, learn the necessity of submitting with humility and grace to the power of the magistrate, and the laws of their country.—Come with me, I have ordered the Chief Justice to meet us in my closet.

*Scene closes.*

The great master of writing, *Shakespeare*, has so admirably sketched the conduct of Prince Henry, with respect to the Lord Chief Justice, that perhaps it may be thought presumption in me even to have attempted the subject; but as he has merely *sketched* it, I thought it not improper to endeavour at filling up an outline, which furnishes so bright an example of self-command and obedience. I cannot, however, resist adding a few of Shakespeare's expressions concerning this circumstance, especially as it is probable the generality of my young readers have not yet been indulged with a perusal of that great author's works. The following is the conversation, founded on history, which he supposes to have passed between the Prince, then King Henry, and the Lord Chief Justice.

### " KING.

*You* are assured, I think, I love you not.

### LORD CHIEF JUSTICE.

I am assured, if I be measured rightly,
Your Majesty has no just cause to hate me.

### KING.

No!—Might a Prince of my great hopes forget
So great indignities you laid upon me?
What rate, rebuke, and roughly send to prison,
The immediate heir of England?—Was this easy!
Might this be wash'd in Lethe, and forgotten?

### CHIEF JUSTICE.

I then did use the person of your father;
The image of his power lay then in me,
And in the administration of his law,
While I was busy for the commonwealth,
Your Highness pleased to forget my place,
The majesty and power of law and justice,
The image of the King whom I presented,
And struck me in my very seat of justice;
Whereon, as an offender to your father,
I gave bold way to my authority,
And did commit you. If the deed be ill,
Be you contented, wearing now the crown,
To have a son set your decrees at nought,
To pluck down justice from your awful bench;

## PRINCE HENRY.

To trip the courſe of law, and blunt the ſword
Which guards the peace and ſafety of your perſon.

### KING.

You are right, Juſtice, and you weigh this well;
Therefore, ſtill bear the balance, and the ſword,
And I do wiſh your honours may increaſe,
'Till you do live to ſee a ſon of mine
Offend you, and obey you, as I did.
———There is my hand,
You ſhall be as a father to my youth, &c. &c."

# THE DISTREST FAMILY.
## A DRAMA.
### IN TWO PARTS.

"Such fate to suffering worth is given,
"Who long with wants and woes has striven;
"By cruel fraud and cunning driven
  "To misery's brink.
"'Till wrench'd of every stay, save Heav'n,
  "He ruin'd sunk."

Poems, by R. Burns.

## PERSONS.

| | |
|---|---|
| Mr. BARCLAY, | |
| ELEONORA, | His Daughter. |
| WILMOT, | A Poor Man. |
| AGNES, | His Sick Wife. |
| JOHNSON, | A Farmer. |
| RACHEL, } | |
| GEORGE, } | Wilmot's Children. |

SCENE *before a Cottage, with a small railed Garden, a distant view of a Village, the Church, &c.—Wilmot comes out of the cottage.*

### WILMOT.

THE Sun is arisen; the mists are partly dispelled.—How pure is the air!—For a moment let me try to forget my my cares, and enjoy thefe refrefhing odours.—(*He paufes.*)—Oh, how vain the attempt!—Thefe fcenes, the moment of day-break, once fo delicious to my heart, to which it ufed to expand with fo much rapture, have loft their power!—Oh, my God, it was here I ufed to offer to thee my morning facrifice of praife and prayer. It was here, foftened into univerfal benevolence, I ufed to pray for all men.—I no longer feel thofe delightful emotions.—A weight of grief hangs upon my heart. The ardour of my devotion is departed. My wifhes are contracted to a point.—I have loft my hopes on earth; and, I fear, I am alfo lofing my truft in God.—Oh, my heavenly father, deign to hear me!—Suffer me not to defpair of thy mercies, or to murmur at thy will!—Teach me to fupport my anguifh, if not with the fortitude of a man, with the refignation of a chriftian! (*He leans againft a tree, with his face on his arms, in thought.*)

RACHEL

RACHEL *enters from the cottage; as she shuts the door, she looks back, and says,*

Be quiet, George—don't make a noise, I shall be back in a minute.

(*She advances.*)

RACHEL, (*taking Wilmot's hand,*)

Father, my dear father, why are you so sad?

WILMOT.

My child!

RACHEL.

Indeed, father, my mother is better. —She sleeps.

WILMOT, (*breaking from her with distraction.*)

She will soon sleep in death!—Must I see her die!—Without friends, without the means of procuring her proper assistance, I see her languishing under a disease which might be cured, could I but obtain proper nourishment for her.—Why do I hesitate!—Driven from men, as if I did not belong to their species, the bands

## THE DISTREST FAMILY. 65

between me and fociety are broken; wherefore then fhould I not fall, like a beaft of prey, on thofe barbarous wretches who leave us to perifh.

RACHEL, (*coming to him.*)

Father, you did not bid me pray to-day, but I have prayed.—Why do you not teach me to be good, as you ufed to do?

WILMOT, (*catching her in his arms.*)

Oh, my child!—My God! thou haft made this innocent my preferver.—Are the bands between me and fociety broken!—Oh no! my children are ties which I dare not break.—Thou haft trufted them to me!—Dare I corrupt thy work, and lead thofe to wickednefs and mifery whom thou haft created to be good and happy?

RACHEL.

What do you mean, father?—Why do you cry—why do you fpeak fo haftily—are you angry with me?

WILMOT.

WILMOT.

No, my child, no!—Happy innocent!—thou knowest not the force of the passions!—thou readest not the anguish of a heart, fluctuating between good and evil.—Go, my child, to thy mother; she may want thee.

RACHEL.

I will, father.—(*As she goes out, she meets Mr. Johnson.—She curtsies, but he takes no notice.*)

RACHEL, (*aside.*)

How cross he looks!—I hope he won't scold my father!—What can make people so cross, I wonder! (*She goes in.*)

WILMOT.

Good-day to you, Sir.

JOHNSON, (*in a rough tone.*)

Servant, George.—What art doing here; why dost not get to work, man?

WILMOT.

Sir, I am going to work; but my wife has

has been ill all night.—I fear for her life.—I know not how to leave her, leaſt I ſhould ſee her no more.

#### JOHNSON.

Well, well, man, if thee doſt not work, thy wife cannot eat, nor thy children neither; that's all I know.

#### WILMOT.

Alas, Sir, I would I were able to work inceſſantly, for their ſakes; would that I could live without reſt, that I might earn more for their ſupport.

#### JOHNSON.

Well, then, why doſt ſtand idle?

#### WILMOT.

Ah, Sir, it is not idleneſs, my ſtrength and my ſpirits fail me, but never my wiſh to labour.

#### JOHNSON.

How thou talk'ſt of thy ſtrength, and thy ſtrength; haſt not as much ſtrength as another?

#### WILMOT.

WILMOT.

At least, Sir, what I have I employ willingly.

JOHNSON.

Don't know that.—Thou dost not as much work in a day and a half, as some of my men do in a day.—George, George, I am afraid thee art lazy; and then thy wife, she is sick.—She says so, however; she can't do this, and she can't do that; her betters can do it.—God knows how you contrive to live!

WILMOT, *(with earnestness.)*

Yes, Sir!—*God does know!*—He sees our hearts; he knows whether or not I wish to work; whether or not my poor Agnes is really sick.—Ah, Heaven, I can bear any thing for myself, but I have not yet learnt to bear reproach on her!

JOHNSON.

Well, well, George, thou seem'st not to be cut out for a working man, thou look'st look'ſt and talk'ſt like a gentleman, ſo may be thou know'ſt how to live like one, I'am ſure I've no objection.

WILMOT, (*aſide.*)

What cruel inſults!—Down proud and rebellious ſpirit.—I will be humble! (*To Johnſon.*)—Ah, Sir, gentlemen do not live as I live; gentlemen do not ſee thoſe they love dying before their eyes, without the power of giving them aſſiſtance.

JOHNSON.

I'll tell thee what, George; if thou can'ſt afford to ſtand chattering here all day, I cannot.—So fare thee well; ſince thou haſt not a mind to work, I muſt find ſomebody who has.

WILMOT.

Good heavens, Sir!—I am going to work inſtantly; do not, I conjure you, do not think of employing another.

JOHNSON.

Well, well, I ſhall ſee about it.

WILMOT.

#### WILMOT.

But, Sir, hear me, I pray you; promise me that you will not employ another.—Consider my poor wife and children.

#### JOHNSON.

'Tis for thee to consider them, and work the harder.

#### WILMOT.

Oh, Sir, you need not fear me; you shall have no reason to complain.

#### JOHNSON.

We shall see that.—Go to work.—The men have been in the fields this half hour. Make haste, and we shall see.

#### WILMOT.

I shall, Sir.   (*Johnson goes out.*)

#### WILMOT.

Oh God!—Oh God!—hear my groans! Pity me, and teach this cruel man to pity me!—Make me forget I ever was, what I am not now!—Oh that I could acquire at once the ſtrength and humility of the hardy peaſant!—My blood riſes, my heart ſwells; hardly could I reſtrain myſelf from anſwering this tyrant as he deſerved.—Let me ſee my Agnes once more, and then haſten to obey this imperious maſter.

*(He goes into the cottage, then comes out again, croſſes the ſtage, and goes out. Rachel and George follow him.)*

RACHEL.

Good-bye, father, good-bye.—Come, George, let us go and get ſome ſticks, to boil the potatoes.

GEORGE.

But mother will want you.

RACHEL.

No, ſhe ſays ſhe is better.—She will not eat any breakfaſt, however.—She does not like bread.

GEORGE.

I like it—but I like it beſt with an apple.

RACHEL.

###### RACHEL.

Oh, but apples are scarce.—Our tree had but a few, and those must be saved for mother; she can eat a bit now and then.

###### GEORGE.

I am sure, then, I don't want them.—I had rather she had them.

###### RACHEL.

I am sure I wish I could live without eating, that mama might have better things.

###### GEORGE.

*Mama!* You must not say *that*.

###### RACHEL.

Oh, I had forgot; I must never say, mama, since Nancy Johnson laughed at me, and her mother scolded me for saying so.

###### GEORGE.

I hate Nancy Johnson; she's so proud, and ill-temper'd.

###### RACHEL.

RACHEL.

Oh, but you must not hate any body.

GEORGE.

Well, I *will* hate Mrs. Johnson, however, because she's so cross to mother.

RACHEL.

You *will* hate her.—I cannot help laughing at that.

(*While they are laughing, Mr. Barclay and Eleonora come in.*)

ELEONORA.

Dear papa, what pretty children.— What's your name, my dear?

RACHEL, (*curtsying.*)

Rachel Wilmot, ma'am.

ELEONORA.

A very pretty name, and I dare say you are a very good girl.—Is that your brother?

RACHEL.

Yes, ma'am.

ELEONORA.

And what were you laughing at so heartily, my dear?

RACHEL, (*confused.*)

At—at George, ma'am.

ELEONORA.

What did he say, then?

RACHEL.

Ma'am, he says he *will* hate Mrs. Johnson.

MR. BARCLAY, (*laughing.*)

A very kind determination.

RACHEL.

Oh dear, ma'am, but pray don't tell her.—Perhaps you know her.—Pray don't be angry, he is but a child.

ELEONORA.

Be easy, I don't know her; and if I did, I should not tell her.

RACHEL.

Oh, I'am glad of that.—Perhaps it might ruin my father.

MR. BARCLAY.

How so, child?

RACHEL.

Sir, my father works for Mr. Johnson; and, perhaps, they might be affronted.

MR. BARCLAY.

Very likely.—We will not tell them. Be good children—mind your book.— Let me see you at church, and here is six-pence for you.

RACHEL, *(joyfully.)*

Oh dear, Sir, will you be so kind then as to let me work for you.

MR. BARCLAY.

Work, my child!—What work can'st thou do?—Why, do'st think I will give thee work?

RACHEL.

Will you not, Sir?

MR. BARCLAY.

I have none for you, child.

RACHEL.
Then, Sir, what am I to do with this money?

MR. BARCLAY.
Keep it, my child.

RACHEL.
Sir, my father ſays, I muſt not take money till I can work for it.—He forbids me to beg.

MR. BARCLAY.
Charming little creature!

ELEONORA.
How amiable!—But, my dear, you did not beg; my papa gave it to you.

RACHEL.
But I don't think my father would like me to have it.

MR. BARCLAY.
Her integrity is charming!—Look then, my child, I want thoſe flowers which grow yonder.—I will give you ſix-pence to gather them for me.

RACHEL.

### RACHEL.

Oh, yes, Sir, yes.
*(She runs and gathers the flowers. Mr. Barclay gives her the six-pence, and the flowers to Eleonora.)*

### MR. BARCLAY.

Keep them, my Eleonora, and if ever you should be tempted to forget my precepts, let them remind you how well this little cottager kept those of her father.

### ELEONORA.

I can never forget it.—Adieu, Rachel. I shall see you again some time or other.

### RACHEL.

Good-bye, ma'am.—Thank you, Sir.
*(She curtsies. They go out.)*

RACHEL. GEORGE.

### RACHEL.

O, George, see!—I have got sixpence!—I shall go directly to the village, and buy mother some biscuits, such as she likes, and some coffee; I can have both for six-pence.—Go in—don't tell her where I am gone.—If she wants any thing, Dame Green will come, if you call her.—Don't you make a racket.

### GEORGE.

No, no.—Good-bye.

*(Rachel goes out. George goes into the cottage.)*

*Scene closes.*

**END OF THE FIRST PART.**

**PART**

## PART THE SECOND.

SCENE, *the Inside of the Cottage.*
*Agnes, Rachel, George.—A small table stands by Agnes, with coffee and biscuits.—A little inner room is seen, with a bed.*

RACHEL.

BUT, mother, you don't eat the biscuits.

AGNES.

Yes, my dear, I have eaten one; take one yourself.

RACHEL.

No, thank ye, mother.

AGNES.

Why not?

RACHEL.

I am not hungry.

AGNES.

My child, there are more than I can eat; you may take one safely.

RACHEL.

But, mother, they will not be spoiled by to-morrow, and they are better for you than bread.—I like bread very much.

AGNES.

My dear Rachel! (*embraces her with tears.*)—My God, I thank thee for the blessing of such affectionate children; they comfort me in all my distresses! Rachel, see if your father is coming.

RACHEL, (*going to the window.*)

No, mother, it is twelve o'clock too; how very hot it is!

AGNES.

Alas, how my poor Wilmot will be fatigued.—He exhausts his strength in working for us.—I dare not wish to die, for I know how much my death would afflict him!—And my poor children, they yet need a mother's care!

RACHEL.

Mother, my dear mother, why do you cry; my father will soon be here.

GEORGE,

GEORGE, (*at the window.*)
Don't cry, mother, my father is coming.

AGNES.
Do not tell him I have been crying.—I am better now; how near is he?

GEORGE.
Mother, he is just getting over the stile; he looks up to the sky; he wipes his face.—Ah, how hot he is; I will run out to him.   (*He runs out.*)

AGNES.
Ah, how he must be fatigued!—In this burning Sun—he that was so delicately bred!  (*Wimlot and George come in.*)

GEORGE.
Here he is, mother—here he is!

AGNES.
My dear Wilmot!—How tired you are.

RACHEL, (*sets a chair.*)
Sit down here, father; let me take your hat?

##### WILMOT.

The Sun is so hot!—My dear Agnes, how are you?

##### AGNES.

Better, thank you!—Rachel has procured me some coffee; it has done me good.—Take a cup of it, it will refresh you.

##### WILMOT, (*in a low voice.*)

No.

##### AGNES.

What is the matter?—You look pale. Oh, Wilmot, speak to me, for God's sake.—You are ill?—Ah, he is dying. He has killed himself for me!

> (*Wilmot fainting, leans back. Agnes runs for water, and sprinkles him. Rachel and George scream. Rachel runs to the door.*)

##### RACHEL.

Help, help!—Oh, my father is dying. Mother, mother, don't you die too.

##### GEORGE,

The Distrest Family.

Wilmots distress relieved by
Mr and Miss Barclay.

GEORGE, (*crying.*)

Oh, mother, mother!

(*A knocking at the door.—After a while, it is repeated.*)

AGNES.

Wilmot, Wilmot, speak to me, speak to me.

(*The knocking is heard again. Rachel opens the door. Mr. Barclay and Eleonora come in. Agnes still hangs over Wilmot, in the greatest agony.*)

MR. BARCLAY.

What is the matter, good people—What occasioned the screams I heard?

RACHEL.

Oh, Sir, my father is dead, and my mother is dying.—George, George, let us die too!

ELEONORA.

My dear, don't be frighten'd—he is not dead, he will soon recover. (*To Agnes.*) Pray don't be so terrified.

(*Agnes*

(*Agnes looks only at Wilmot. Eleonora takes out her salts; applies them to Wilmot. Mr. Barclay supports him.*)

MR. BARCLAY.

My good woman, recover yourself; he is only faint.

AGNES.

Oh no, he is dead.—I have killed him. Wilmot, I shall not out-live you.

(*Wilmot begins to recover; half raises his head, and looks at Agnes.—In a moment he speaks.*)

WILMOT.

My wife!

AGNES.

I am here—I am at your side.—I will not leave you, even in death.

WILMOT.

My dearest Agnes, I am better; do not terrify yourself.

ELEONORA.

Indeed there is no need—he will be well presently.

WILMOT.

#### WILMOT.

Ah, madam, I beg your pardon.—I fear I have been troublesome to you?

#### ELEONORA.

By no means; your wife and children have been sadly alarmed.—Pray prevail on your wife to take some care of herself.

#### WILMOT.

Agnes, I entreat you to sit down.

ELEONORA, (*placing her in a chair.*)
Take a little water, will you?—Rachel, shew me where it is, I will fetch some.

(*She fetches water, and obliges Agnes to drink of it, who is relieved by a violent fit of crying.*)

#### AGNES.

Thank you, ma'am, you are extremely good.

#### MR. BARCLAY.

Have you been ill long, my friend?

#### WILMOT.

No, Sir, I was very well this morning.

###### AGNES.

Ah, my dear Wilmot, you have overworked yourself.—This burning Sun—Your cares, your anxiety, have overcome you!—Why would you do so?

###### WILMOT.

My dear Agnes, if you knew the terrors I have suffered!

###### MR. BARCLAY.

The terrors!

###### WILMOT.

Yes, Sir, of being deprived of my work. My master threatened me this morning with dismission; he accuses me of laziness.

###### AGNES.

Oh, what you!—You who have worked so eagerly, so constantly?

###### WILMOT.

Alas, yes!—Unable before to procure for you, my dear Agnes, the support your disease required, could I bear the idea of losing the common necessaries for you,

and

and for my children?—Nor was this all, the cruel man added the moſt bitter and unprovoked reflections on me, and thoſe I love beſt.—I left you, Agnes, this morning half heart broken, and ſcarcely able to reſolve on longer enduring a miſerable exiſtence, except for thoſe dear ſakes, whoſe remembrance urged me on beyond my ſtrength!

AGNES.

Ah, Wilmot, to us then you owe your illneſs, even perhaps your death; to us who would have died to ſave you!

GEORGE.

Father, let me help you work tomorrow; perhaps Mr. Johnſon won't ſcold then.

WILMOT.

Alas, my child!

MR. BARCLAY.

Pray tell me, who is this oppreſſive man, this Johnſon, of whom you ſpeak?

WILMOT.

Sir, he is the farmer who employs me.

MR. BAR-

MR. BARCLAY.
Where does he live?

WILMOT.
In a farm, called Oatley, Sir.

MR. BARCLAY.
I thought so.—It is my farm, and he is now urging me for a new lease, on terms very favourable to himself.—I am glad to learn how I ought to deal with him.

WILMOT.
I should be sorry, Sir, to prejudice you against him; he is honest, and a good farmer.

MR. BARCLAY.
You do yourself honour, by thus repaying his unkindness; but he must not expect *me* to favour a man capable of such conduct.

AGNES.
I beg your pardon, ma'am, for not asking you to sit down.—We are exceedingly indebted to you for the trouble you have taken.

ELEONORA.

##### ELEONORA.

Not in the least.—I would not be impertinent; but—can we be of service to you?

##### WILMOT, (*aside.*)

Vain prejudice, which has so long taught me to conceal my distresses, begone!—Unable longer to labour, I must apply to the compassion of others, Sir.

##### MR. BARCLAY.

Speak freely, my good friend.—Can I assist you?

##### WILMOT.

Ah, Sir, the dear woman you see has been ill a long time; she is better, but her weak state requires nourishment, which I cannot procure for her.

##### AGNES.

My dear Wilmot, think more of yourself, and less of me.—It is he, Sir, who requires your assistance.—I have already taken refreshment, which your kindness this morning enabled my child to procure.

MR. BARCLAY.
What! my little flower-gatherer!—Amiable child!

ELEONORA.
My good friend, your husband seems much recovered; you are yourself indisposed, be prevailed on to lie down; in the mean time my father will learn how he can be of use to you.

WILMOT.
Do, my dear Agnes; I am quite well.

AGNES.
Since you request it, I will obey you.

ELEONORA.
Let me help you?

AGNES.
Oh no!—dear young lady, I cannot bear you should wait on me.

ELEONORA.
Why not?—It is a pleasure to me.

AGNES.
But it is giving you so much trouble.

ELEONORA.

### ELEONORA.

Not at all.—I dare say, if I were sick, and you were well, you would wait on me?

### AGNES.

Most surely.—It would be fit I should be your servant.

### ELEONORA.

To be sure, it is always fit those who are in health should wait on those who are sick.

### AGNES.

What sweetness!

(*She goes out, leaning on Eleonora, followed by Rachel; in a minute Eleonora returns.*)

ELEONORA, (*in a low voice, to her father.*)

Sir, these poor people have great need of refreshment, let me fetch it from home, I will return presently.

### MR. BARCLAY.

Do so, but do not run, it is too hot.

### ELEONORA.

ELEONORA.

I will not.

(*Mr. Barclay, Wilmot. George at a diſtance.*)

MR. BARCLAY.

My child will ſoon return; ſhe is gone for refreſhment.

WILMOT.

Ah, Sir, how can I thank you for your goodneſs!

MR. BARCLAY.

My good friend, why would you not apply to me before?

WILMOT.

Sir, while I was able, by the work of my hands, to procure for my wife and children the means of life, I had no right to encroach upon the goodneſs of others, or on that relief which poorer wretches had a better right to.—But when my ſtrength failed me; when I ſaw myſelf on the point of being deprived of work,

and

and my children of bread, it became time to aſk, and God has been pleaſed that I ſhould not aſk in vain.

MR. BARCLAY.

I admire your ſentiments, and——

RACHEL *enters.*

RACHEL.

Father, my mother is inclined to ſleep, but every time her eyes cloſe ſhe ſtarts and fancies ſhe ſees you fainting again.— If you go to her, perhaps, ſhe will be eaſy.

WILMOT.

Sir ———

MR. BARCLAY.

Go, my friend, no apologies; I will chat awhile with Rachel; I ſhall tell you a charming ſtory of her.

(*Wilmot goes in. Rachel ſtands by Mr. Barclay.*)

RACHEL.

Will my mother get well ſoon, Sir, do you think?

MR. BARCLAY.

I hope so, my dear; has she been ill long?

RACHEL.

Oh yes, Sir, a great while; all the winter she had a cough, but it is gone; but she is so weak, and then she cannot eat bread and potatoes, as we do.—I bought her some coffee to-day, with the money I had from you, Sir.—She took some.—I was so pleased!—But my father frighted us sadly!

MR. BARCLAY.

Did you ever see him so before?

RACHEL.

No, Sir; he is often tired very much indeed, but not so bad.—To be sure, he has not been used to such hard work.

MR. BARCLAY.

What work then has he been used to, my child?

RACHEL.

### RACHEL.

Why, Sir, it is great while ago, before George can remember, we lived in a nice houſe, and had ſervants, and I had white frocks, and fine people uſed to come and ſee us!—But now the fine people don't come, Sir; why don't they?

### MR. BARCLAY.

Happy innocent!—Thou knoweſt not how eagerly the great fly from the unfortunate!

(*Eleonora returns with a baſket.*)

### MR. BARCLAY.

My dear!—What, have you carried that baſket thro' the heat?

### ELEONORA.

No, Sir, I thought you would not be pleaſed, ſo I made John bring it to the gate, but I would not let him come in, for theſe people ſeem to have ſo much feeling, I could not bear to bring an unneceſſary witneſs of their diſtreſs.

MR. BARCLAY, (*embracing her.*)
My dear girl!

ELEONORA.
Rachel, see if your mother is asleep.
(*Rachel goes into the inner room. Wilmot comes out.*)

WILMOT.
My poor Agnes can get no rest.

ELEONORA.
I will go to her.—I have brought some drops, which will compose her spirits.
(*She takes cut of the basket a bottle of wine, two glasses, slices of cold ham, and bread and cakes.*)

ELEONORA.
Papa, will you eat something?—Perhaps Mr. Wilmot will take a glass of wine.

WILMOT, (*aside.*)
Charming delicacy!—How I feel that kindness!

*Eleonora*

(*Eleonora goes into the inner room. Mr. Barclay and Wilmot fit at the table. Rachel and George creep towards them. Mr. Barclay gives them cakes. They all eat.*)

WILMOT, (*looking after Eleonora.*)

Angelic charity!—Not contented with furnifhing the means of health, fhe adminifters them herfelf, waiting with humility and fweetnefs on the poor and wretched!

MR. BARCLAY.

There is nothing extraordinary in that; can one know what it is to be ill, and leave thofe who are fo to the unfeeling attendance of fervants, or mercenary nurfes?

WILMOT.

No; *you* cannot.—Warm and feeling, your hearts make the diftreffes of others your own.

MR. BARCLAY.

That is no matter of wonder.

###### WILMOT.

Oh! not to *you*.—Goodnefs is to you too common to be wonderful.—But to *me*, to *me* who have been rejected by the world, caft off by my relations, fuch kindnefs is fcarcely credible!

###### MR. BARCLAY.

Your lot feems to have been an hard one, but let it not make you think ill of all mankind.

###### MR. BARCLAY.

There feems to be fomething uncommon in your ftory, and if the recital be not painful——

###### WILMOT.

The recital, Sir, I thank God, will not be painful, for I have no guilt of my own to relate.

###### MR. BARCLAY.

I dare engage it.

###### WILMOT.

Perhaps, of fome imprudence, you will not

not so easily acquit me.—I was born to a good estate; just after I came of age, my father died; soon after, I married that dear woman you have seen.—She was of good family, but had no fortune; mine was sufficient for us both, but fond as I was of my Agnes, desiring to procure for her every indulgence, I lived to the extent of my income, and far beyond her wishes: for five years we lived happily, when a distant relation of the person from whom my father had bought the estate, pretending a fault in the title, laid claim to it; the cause was tried, and by an artifice my chief witness kept out of court. I lost my cause, and was left destitute; my relations excusing themselves on account of my marrying, as they called it, imprudently, and my living expensively, refused me any assistance, and, with the rest of my friends, turned their backs upon me.

MR. BARCLAY.

What cruel conduct!

WILMOT.

#### WILMOT.

One friend alone was left, who received us into his houſe, and would have procured a re-hearing of our cauſe, but he died, and we were ſent forth to wander through the world. I hired this cottage, where, by the labour of my hands, I have ſupported my wife, that dear conſoling angel, who has never once reproached me for the miſery I have brought upon her, and our children; till her ſickneſs drove me almoſt to diſtraction and deſpair, from which Heaven ſent you this day to relieve me.

#### MR. BARCLAY.

Make yourſelf eaſy, I hope all will be well; our firſt care muſt be to reſtore your wife.—Is the perſon yet alive who was to have witneſſed in your cauſe?

#### WILMOT.

He is.

#### MR. BARCLAY.

Very well. My dear Wilmot hear me,
I am

I am tolerably rich, I have only one child, I will support you in this cause; if, on enquiry, I find you are likely to succeed, and I will only ask in return your promise to repay me when you regain your estate.

#### WILMOT.

Sir—such amazing kindness to a stranger!

#### MR. BARCLAY.

No, Wilmot, not to a stranger. I knew your father well; he was my senior at college. I have often heard of this cause as a most iniquitous transaction, and I have no doubt of your success, so that all the favour I do you is to advance you a little money; no mighty obligation!

#### WILMOT.

Oh yes!—My obligations to you *are* mighty, are not to be repaid!—Best of men!

#### MR. BARCLAY.

Psha! there are thousands better.

#### WILMOT.

Such amazing generofity!

#### MR. BARCLAY.

There is really no generofity in the matter.—I am fure of my fecurity.

#### WILMOT.

What, Sir!—The word of a perfon you do not know!

#### MR. BARCLAY.

No, Wilmot, not of a perfon I do not know.—I have feen enough of you to convince me you are honeft and grateful; what better fecurity fhould I defire?

#### WILMOT.

I am over-powered!—My children, blefs your benefactor!

#### RACHEL.

Oh, Sir, will you make my father and mother well and happy?

#### GEORGE.

And will you give my mother fome-thing better to eat than potatoes?

WILMOT.

#### WILMOT.

Oh yes, my children, he will save us all.—Thank him then; learn to love and serve him; keep about you—never forget the form of this cottage; and if, as I hope, we live to inhabit a better place, remember always who rescued us from poverty!

#### MR. BARCLAY.

No more, no more; if you will think yourself obliged to me, in return do me the favour not to thank me.

*(Eleonora enters softly.*

#### ELEONORA.

Mr. Wilmot, your wife is asleep; she will be well, I dare say—and you, how are you?

#### WILMOT.

Oh, well, quite well!—The blessing of Heaven accompanies you; all must be well where you are.

##### MR. BARCLAY.

Wilmot, think of what I have said to you. In the evening I will send my carriage to bring you all to my house, where you shall remain, either till your cause is gained, or, if that cannot be, till I can place you in some way of life better suited to your birth. (*To Eleonara.*) My dear, Mr. Wilmot is entitled to a very large fortune, which I hope to procure for him.

##### ELEONORA.

I am very glad of it, but fortune cannot add to my respect for people so worthy.

##### WILMOT.

Angelic creature!—How can I ever want——

##### MR. BARCLAY.

You forget my injunctions!—I shall send for you—be ready.—In the mean time, take care of yourselves.

##### RACHEL.

#### RACHEL.

What, father, shall we ride in a coach?

#### ELEONORA.

Yes, my dear, often, every day, if you continue good; and, what is better, you shall have a great many charming little books.

#### RACHEL.

Oh, how glad I shall be.

#### MR. BARCLAY.

Wilmot, farewell!

#### ELEONORA.

Farewell, Mr. Wilmot.—Good-bye, Rachel; we shall expect you.

#### WILMOT.

Every blessing attend you!

#### RACHEL.

Thank you, thank you.

*(She kisses Eleonora's hand, who embraces her.—Wilmot attends Mr. Barclay to the door, and returns.)*

WILMOT.

Oh, my God!—How can I ever thank thee, for such amazing goodness!—Heart broken, wearied, on the point of renouncing my dependance on thee; of setting thy laws at defiance; *that* moment hast thou chosen to relieve and bless me!—Aweful and striking lesson!—Shall I ever again despair, when I know that the next hour to that of our greatest misery may bring with it comfort and happiness!—I hear my Agnes coming; let me meet and explain to her these happy events!

*Scene closes.*

The limits of the Drama not allowing of the events being finished, it may perhaps be satisfactory to the reader to hear, that Mrs. Wilmot recovered; and that Wilmot, gaining his cause, by Mr. Barclay's means, was restored to affluence, and the two families formed a friendship, which lasted during their lives.

# THE VILLAGE WEDDING.

## A DRAMA.

### IN ONE PART.

---

"Bless'd too is he whose evening ramble strays
"Where droop the sons of indigence and care;
"His little gift their gladden'd eyes amaze,
"And win at small expence their fondest pray'r."
                                        SHENSTONE.

---

| | |
|---|---|
| LORD AUBREY, | LORD OF THE MANOR. |
| COLONEL NESBIT, | |
| LADY AUBREY, } | HIS DAUGHTERS. |
| MISS NESBIT, } | |
| ROBERT, | AN OLD PEASANT. |
| LUCETTA, | HIS DAUGHTER. |
| PHILIP, | MARRIED TO LUCETTA. |
| PEASANTS. | |

SCENE, *a Lawn before a Cottage.*

*(Under the shade of some trees a table is spread, with fruits, milk, and cyder. Robert, and some old peasants, sit at this table. Philip, Lucetta, and some young peasants, are dancing on the lawn. Lucetta is dressed in white, with flowers, as a bride. Philip as a bridegroom.*

### ROBERT.

AYE, marry neighbour, it does my heart good to see them.—Look 'ye ye there, I'll warrant ye as light as the best!

#### OLD PEASANT.

Truly, neighbour Robert, Lucetta is a pretty girl; yes, yes, you may well be proud of her. She is not only handsome, but good.

#### ROBERT.

Ah, neighbour!—She is the joy of my old heart!—Had her mother lived to see this day!   (*He wipes his eyes.*)

#### OLD PEASANT.

Come cheerly, neighbour, don't let's disturb ourselves with sad thoughts, we met to be merry.

(*Lucetta seeing her father look sad, runs out of the dance.*)

#### LUCETTA.

Ah, father!—What's the matter?—You are not ill?

#### ROBERT.

No, no, my child, I am very well, and very happy.

#### LUCETTA.

#### LUCETTA.

Well, then!—why look sad!—on my wedding-day too!—Truly, I will not excuse it!  (*He smiles.*)

ROBERT, (*taking her in his arms.*)
My child, I do not weep for sorrow, but for joy, thou art so good, and so happy.

#### LUCETTA.

Ah, my dear father, I owe both to you!—but not a single tear must you shed to-day.—Ah, ha, here comes Philip; he thinks something is the matter.

(*She runs to Philip, gives him her hand, he leads her back to the dance.*)

#### OLD PEASANT.

Aye, aye, they are happy enough!—Well, they be a sweet couple.

#### OLD WOMAN.

As to Lucetta, I must say, I don't know her equal, nor ever did, except my poor daughter, that's gone.—Marry, neigh-

neighbour Robert, I have reaſon to love your girl; how kind ſhe was to me, when my poor daughter lay ſick.—Don't grieve ſo, neighbour Martha, ſhe would ſay, pray don't; I'll do all I can to fill your daughter's place.—Ah, and ſo ſhe has; ſhe tended me when I was ſick; ſhe works for me, now my eye-ſight fails! Ah, marry, I love her as if ſhe was my own!

### SECOND OLD WOMAN.

Then ſhe is ſo kind to the children; my little grand-daughters run when they ſee her coming—here's Lucetta, they ſay, here's Lucetta; truly, 'tis a holiday to ſee her!

### ROBERT.

Ah, it does my heart good, to hear her praiſes!—What a bleſſed thing it is to have every-body's good word!

### OLD PEASANT.

Aye, Robert, that's the honeſt man's reward, to be well thought of himſelf, and leave a good name to his children!

### ROBERT.

#### ROBERT.

True, neighbour, true; but look, here's gentlefolks. Marry, 'tis our young Lord, and his bride.

#### OLD WOMAN.

Yes, and that is my Lady's father, and her sister.—Mercy! how handsome they be!

*Enter* LORD *and* LADY AUBREY, COLONEL *and* MISS NESBIT.

#### LADY AUBREY.

What a charming scene!—How happy these good people seem!

#### COLONEL NESBIT.

This appears to be a wedding.

#### MISS NESBIT.

Ah, that is the bride!—What a pretty creature, and how neat.

#### LORD AUBREY.

That young man is the bridegroom, I fancy; how happy he looks!

### COLONEL NESBIT.
Ah!—I see the bride's father!

### LADY AUBREY.
Where, Sir?

### COLONEL NESBIT.
The old peasant, seated under the shade of those trees, and surrounded by his neighbours.—I know him by the joy, the happiness of his looks!—yes, I am well acquainted with the sweet transports of beholding a daughter happily married.

### LADY AUBREY, (*kissing his hand.*)
Ah, my dear father, your heart has led you to him.

(*They advance; the old people rise up.*)

### LORD AUBREY.
Keep your seats, my good friends.—We are willing to share with you, but not to interrupt this happy scene.

### ROBERT.
Won't your Lordship, and my good Lady, please to sit down?

### THE VILLAGE WEDDING.

**LORD AUBREY.**

No, thank you, my old friend, we will stand nearer the dancers; I love to see them.

**LADY AUBREY.**

We shall go away, if we interrupt you, good people; pray take your seats again.

**ROBERT.**

Thank your good Ladyship.
*(Lord Aubrey, Lady Aubrey, and Miss Nesbit, walk towards the dancers.)*

**COLONEL NESBIT.**

My honest friends, with your leave, I shall sit with you.—We will leave the young folks to themselves; we old ones can but look on now, though some years ago we could have danced with the best of them.

**ROBERT.**

Your Honour is all goodness.
*(He gives a chair. Col. Nesbit sits down, the Peasants seem to hesitate.)*

###### COLONEL NESBIT.

Come, come, sit down all of you; I insist upon it.

*(They sit. Robert and the Colonel a little apart from the rest.)*

###### COLONEL NESBIT.

So, my good friend, this is a wedding, is it?

###### ROBERT.

Yes, your Honour; and I pray God it may prove a happy one.

###### COLONEL NESBIT.

I don't doubt it.—That is the bride, I suppose; a pretty girl, truly.—I must drink to her health.

###### ROBERT.

Sir, you do her honour.

###### COLONEL NESBIT.

I need not be told she is your daughter. I read in your face how much you are concerned in this affair.

###### ROBERT.

## THE VILLAGE WEDDING. 115

#### ROBERT.

Ah, Sir, 'tis an affair of confequence, indeed!—The marrying an only and dear child, is no light matter.

#### COLONEL NESBIT.

Moſt ſurely not; and, I dare ſay, you have taken care to marry her well.

#### ROBERT.

Yes, your Honour, well; I *hope* well. Philip is a worthy, good young man.—He has been brought up in this village; I have known him ever ſince he was half the height of my ſtick, as I may ſay. —A good tempered lad.—" Neighbour, ſhall I do this for you; ſhall I do that.— Neighbour, I am going to market; can I do any thing for you?" All that makes one love a lad.

#### COLONEL NESBIT.

No doubt.

#### ROBERT.

At laſt, Sir, I began to find out he liked my daughter.—That made me think a little.

little.—Lucetta, they say, is pretty.—I know she is good; and farmer Thomas, who is main rich, had made her an offer, but the girl did not like him.—Marry, I can't say he is one of the best.—But I tire your Honour.

### COLONEL NESBIT.

Not at all, my friend, not at all, I take pleasure in hearing you.

### ROBERT.

Your Honour is very kind.—To be sure, Philip is poor; and I cannot give my girl much: 'tis hard, your Honour, to fear one shall live to see one's children want!—But then, I bethought me that Philip is an industrious lad; and Lucetta knows how to manage very prettily.— " Father, (said Philip) if you give me Lucetta, don't fear while I have strength but we shall do very well.—I'll work for her while I can, and when I can work no longer, 1 hope God will take care of us." What could I say, your Honour?
I could

I could not refuse him, and so this morning they were married.

**COLONEL NESBIT.**

You have done very right, my friend, and this must be a happy day to you.

**ROBERT.**

Ah, Sir, it is a happy day!—But yet not without its cares.—I cannot think of the future without some fear!—But I rely on Providence, and hope it will support a virtuous young couple, who will not spend their days in idleness.

**COLONEL NESBIT.**

Good old man!—you need fear nothing.—Hear me, my friend!—I am a father myself; I have lately experienced what it is to marry away a daughter, dearer far dearer than my life.—I know the cares, the anxieties of a father for the happiness of his child; but I cannot endure the idea of your suffering a care which I can remove so easily.—My good friend,

friend, I cannot enfure your child's future happinefs; but, at leaft, I can contribute to it, and to your eafe, by removing your fears of future poverty for her. Happily, as I have married my daughter with wealth beyond her wants or wifhes, I cannot permit a man, a father like myfelf, to ftruggle with a fear fo painful, as that of his daughter's future fubfiftence. (*He takes out his pocket-book.*) My good friend, take thefe notes; this is worth an hundred pounds, this is worth fifty; the fum they will produce will fufficiently fupport you in your old age, and your children when death obliges you to quit them.

#### ROBERT.

But, your Honour—what—I do not underftand.

#### COLONEL NESBIT.

My good old man, thefe notes are yours.—Do me the favour to accept them.

#### ROBERT.

The Village Wedding.

Col.ˡ Nesbit presenting a Wedding portion to the Old Peasant for his Daughter.

###### ROBERT.

Oh Heavens!—What goodness!—Is this possible!—Surely I dream!

###### COLONEL NESBIT.

Ah, virtuous old man, let us not think a common act of kindness so extraordinary as to disbelieve its reality!

###### ROBERT.

Ah, Sir!—a *common* act!

###### COLONEL NESBIT.

Let us say no more of it!—The notes are yours; and, believe me, I feel more pleasure in giving than you do in receiving them.—You will, perhaps, chuse to purchase a little farm; which may descend to your children's children.

###### ROBERT.

Ah, yes, Sir, and they shall learn to bless your name, to honour your goodness!—In spring, when they see the opening blossoms; in autumn, when they
gather

gather in harveſt; they ſhall, next to their God, love and bleſs your name.

### COLONEL NESBIT.

My good old friend!—let me not hear any more of this.—I wiſh not to draw obſervation.

(*Lord and Lady Aubrey, Miſs Neſbit, and Lucetta, come towards them.*)

### LADY AUBREY.

What is the matter, my dear Sir?—you ſeem affected.

### LUCETTA.

Father, what is the matter—I ſaw you change colour.

### ROBERT.

Yes, my child!—Come hither, Lucetta—all my cares for thee are at an end!—His Honour!—Oh, beſt of men?

### MISS NESBIT.

What does all this mean?

### LADY AUBREY.

Tell us, my dear Sir—explain the cause of this good man's emotion.

### COLONEL NESBIT.

Nothing, my children; nothing, my friend.

### ROBERT.

Ah, Sir, pardon me, if I disobey you. Look here, my good Lord; see Ladies!—His Honour has most liberally blessed me! *(He shews the notes.)*

### LADY AUBREY.

Ah, my dear father, what goodness!

### COLONEL NESBIT.

Dear Julia!—Blest as I am in my children, happy as I feel in your marriage, could I bear to see a father full of care, which I could so easily relieve?
*(Lady Aubrey throws herself into his arms, while Miss Nesbit kisses his hand.)*

### LADY AUBREY.

My father, how my heart thanks you!

### COLONEL NESBIT.

Silly girls!—What is there in all this to excite surprize?

### LORD AUBREY.

No, my dear Sir, acts of goodness are with you too common to excite surprize; but I am *angry* with you.

### LADY AUBREY.

How!

### LORD AUBREY.

Yes, my dear Julia, your father has invaded *our* rights.—We ought to assist and encourage such of our tenants as are deserving.—My good Robert well merits our attention, and your father shall not rob us of the pleasure of assisting him.

### LADY AUBREY.

I am quite of your opinion.

### THE VILLAGE WEDDING. 123

COLONEL NESBIT.

So, so, I am to be chid amongst you, it seems.

LORD AUBREY.

Not if you will permit us to join your benevolent intentions.

COLONEL NESBIT.

Oh, with all my heart.

>*(During this conversation, Robert, Philip, and Lucetta, with great marks of pleasure and surprize, have been looking at the notes, and talking apart.)*

LORD AUBREY.

Come hither, my friends?

ROBERT.

Yes, my Lord.    *(They advance.)*

LORD AUBREY.

My good Robert, I remember you many years, and from that remembrance, as well as the general report, I know you to be a worthy industrious man.—Had I

been

been earlier at the Park, I ſhould have known of this wedding before hand, and I ſhould have thought it my duty to give you ſomething towards your daughter's portion.—It is not yet too late.—Therefore, I promiſe you half a dozen ſheep, two cows, two pigs, and a ſtock of poultry, provided you make Lucetta the manager of your farm-yard.

###### ROBERT.

Oh Heavens!—I am overpowered.

###### LORD AUBREY.

As to you, Philip, when a man is married, he ought to have a houſe for his wife; you ſhall therefore have the tenement next to Robert's, with the field behind it; for the firſt year it ſhall be rent-free, after which we will agree on ſuch a rent as you will find yourſelf able to pay, and that becauſe I do not deſire to ſet you above the neceſſity of being induſtrious.

###### ROBERT.

###### ROBERT.

Thank you, my Lord, for *that*, more than all the rest.

###### PHILIP.

Oh, my Lord!—I cannot thank you as I ought. (*He runs to Lucetta, takes her by the hand, and says*) thank God, Lucetta, I have a home for thee.—Ah, my dear, help me to thank our noble landlord.

(*They go towards Lord Aubrey, and attempt to throw themselves at his feet; he prevents them.*)

###### LADY AUBREY, (*wiping her eyes.*)

See, sister, how *malicious* they are!—They want to prevent our having a share in their pleasure!—But it remains for us, my pretty Lucetta, to furnish your house, and to give you a stock of groceries.

###### MISS NESBIT.

You are right, sister; and of that satisfaction we will not be deprived.

LUCETTA, (*throwing herself at Lady Aubrey's feet, and kissing her hand.*)

Forgive my boldness, my Lady; I can only thank you by my tears!

(*Lady Aubrey raises and embraces her.*)

ROBERT, (*lifting up his hands and eyes.*)

Oh, my God! these are thy blessings, and I thank thee with sincerity and truth! beseeching thee to render my benefactors as happy during life as I am at this moment!

COLONEL NESBIT.

Good old man, we are debtors to you for the kindness of your prayers!—But we have interrupted your amusements; we will depart.

LORD AUBREY.

Let us see you at the Park, to dinner, to-morrow.

LADY AUBREY.

Ah, Laura, I wish we could teach some of

of our London friends how much more exquisite is the pleasure derived from an evening like this, than from being shut up in a room with wax-lights and cards, or even in the Opera or Play-house.

#### LORD AUBREY.

Farewell, my good friends, continue your mirth.

#### ROBERT.

Our blessings attend your Lordship, and your noble friends.

#### LUCETTA *and* PHILIP.

Heartily, indeed!

#### LADY AUBREY.

Farewell, Lucetta!

*(They go out, and after a dance of the Peasants, the Scene closes.)*

# CHARLES THE FIRST.

## AN HISTORICAL DRAMA.

### IN TWO PARTS.

"He was a man more finn'd againft, than finning."
SHAKESPEARE.

### PERSONS.

CHARLES THE FIRST,
FAIRFAX, { GENERAL of the Parliament Army.
BISHOP JUXON,
COLONEL TOMLINSON,
HERBERT, THE KING'S SERVANT.
DUKE OF GLOUCESTER, The KING'S YOUNG SON.
PRINCESS ELIZABETH, The KING'S DAUGHTER.

SCENE, *St. James's.*

COLONEL TOMLINSON. BISHOP JUXON.

COLONEL.

GOOD-day to you, my reverend Lord, you come with your ufual piety, to prepare the mind of my Royal Prifoner for the fpeedy execution of his sentence.

JUXON.

#### JUXON.

Yes, Sir.—I come, hoping, by the affiftance of God, and the King's happy ftate of mind, to prepare him for quitting the world like himfelf.

#### COLONEL.

Ah, my Lord, I am overcome with the virtues and royal manners of my prifoner.—I fee in him, indeed, more faint-like graces than in any of his judges!

#### JUXON.

Miftaken men!—Can they believe themfelves poffeffed of fuperior virtues, who have already fanctioned by their authority, and will foon caufe to be executed, the moft favage murder England ever witneffed!—Where is the King?

#### COLONEL.

He is ftill afleep.—Undifturbed by the noife which is made in preparing his fcaffold,

fold; he sleeps with the most tranquillity!*

JUXON.

Just God!—That great, that virtuous soul, will soon seek its reward with thee!

COLONEL.

Ah, my Lord, doubtless his reward will be glorious.—His errors, expiated by his death, and forgotten in his virtues, future times shall recall his name with pity and reverence; and we, who have witnessed his gracious demeanor, will ever lament him!

JUXON.

Your testimony, Colonel, is noble, and will be the more believed, because you are his enemy.

COLONEL.

I am so no longer.—His majestic and tranquil behaviour, at his trial, has over-

* See Hume's History of England—reign of Charles the First.

come me; and I deeply regret the share I have had in his misfortunes.

#### JUXON.

I believe, Sir, you are not the only person.

#### COLONEL.

No, my Lord, the gallant Fairfax now, with honour, sees himself involved in a crime of which he had no idea.—He vainly struggles to disengage himself; Cromwell has spread his toils too closely.

#### JUXON.

You speak, Sir, so freely, that should Cromwell——

#### COLONEL.

Ah, my Lord, I know to whom I speak!—Would to Heaven it were not yet too late for me to save, at the hazard of my own life, the life of my King!— But, alas!—his guards!—Cromwell's spies——

### JUXON.

It is, indeed, impossible!—We yield to the will of Heaven!—But, Fairfax!—his power?

### COLONEL.

I fear it can do nothing.—Cromwell's deep art has over-reached him.—He meant but to correct, not kill.

### JUXON.

He is, indeed, the Brutus of these conspirators.

> All the Conspirators, save only he,
> Did that they did in envy to great Cæsar;
> He only in a general honest thought,
> And common good to all, made one of them.*

### COLONEL.

You praise him justly, my Lord—And his noble Lady!—What a heart is there! The pure blood which runs in her veins rises in indignation against these regicides; which lately, at the hazard of her life, she avowed.

* Shakespeare's Julius Cæsar.

### JUXON.

come me; and I deeply regret the share I have had in his misfortunes.

#### JUXON.

I believe, Sir, you are not the only person.

#### COLONEL.

No, my Lord, the gallant Fairfax now, with honour, sees himself involved in a crime of which he had no idea.—He vainly struggles to disengage himself; Cromwell has spread his toils too closely.

#### JUXON.

You speak, Sir, so freely, that should Cromwell——

#### COLONEL.

Ah, my Lord, I know to whom I speak!—Would to Heaven it were not yet too late for me to save, at the hazard of my own life, the life of my King!—But, alas!—his guards!—Cromwell's spies——

#### JUXON.

It is, indeed, impoffible!—We yield to the will of Heaven!—But, Fairfax!—his power?

#### COLONEL.

I fear it can do nothing.—Cromwell's deep art has over-reached him.—He meant but to correct, not kill.

#### JUXON.

He is, indeed, the Brutus of thefe confpirators.

> All the Confpirators, fave only he,
> Did that they did in envy to great Cæfar;
> He only in a general honeft thought,
> And common good to all, made one of them.*

#### COLONEL.

You praife him juftly, my Lord—And his noble Lady!—What a heart is there! The pure blood which runs in her veins rifes in indignation againft thefe regicides; which lately, at the hazard of her life, fhe avowed.

* Shakefpeare's Julius Cæfar.

#### JUXON.

#### JUXON.

I do not understand you.

#### COLONEL.

No, my Lord!—Do you not know, that at the trial———

#### JUXON.

I was unable to be there; and many circumstances have escaped my knowledge.

#### COLONEL.

Oh, my Lord, then you saw not the noblest display of magnanimity and mildness this kingdom ever witnessed.

#### JUXON.

I do believe it.—Be pleased to tell me the particulars.

#### COLONEL.

Willingly, my Lord.—They are so impressed upon my memory, I never can forget them.—My Royal Prisoner, with a determined smiling countenance, prepared

pared to hear his accufation.—When they called over the names of his Judges, no anfwer was made to that of Fairfax; a voice from a diftant box exclaimed, *" he has more wit than to be here!"*—A paufe followed, and they proceeded with the accufation, which was framed in the name of the People of England.—The fame voice then cried, *" not the tenth part of them!"* Enraged at this boldnefs, orders were then given to fire into the box; which Axtell prepared to obey, when it was difcovered that the voice proceeded from the noble Lady Fairfax, whofe eager feelings had fo far over-ftepped the timidity of her fex, and impelled her to this public difavowal of their meafures.

JUXON.

Noble Lady!—Never fhall this fad ftory be told hereafter, but with the mention of her name; and many a female heart fhall beat with joy and pride, that

fuch

such virtuous warmth of feeling dwelt in a woman's bosom!

COLONEL.

The King, as your Lordship knows, refused to plead before a Court whose right to judge him he would not allow. Some of the soldiers were prevailed on to call for Justice.

JUXON.

Justice!—prostituted term?

COLONEL.

The King then, turning to Herbert, who was behind him, said, with a smile, in which neither contempt or bitterness had place, " Poor souls! they would do " as much against their Commanders for " a piece of silver!

JUXON.

Oh! glorious effort of Christian humility!

COLONEL.

#### COLONEL.

Alas, my Lord, he had yet more to endure!—As he returned through the foldiers, fome of them, I blufh to relate! with infolent barbarity, dared to fpit in his face; he mildly cried, " my Saviour " bore more than this!"—One foldier, overcome, bleffed him, as he paffed: his cruel Officer inftantly ftruck the fellow to the ground; the King calmly faid, " methinks the punifhment is great, for " fo fmall an offence!"

#### JUXON.

With what joy do I hear thefe inftances of his happy frame of mind!—He is fit to die; and our lofs is all we have to bewail.—See he comes.

*Enter the* KING.

#### KING.

Good-morrow, my good Juxon.—I rife late this morning; you have waited for me?

#### JUXON.

#### JUXON.

I am happy to hear your Majesty sleeps so well.

#### KING.

*Well*, my kind Juxon!—never better. My mind sleeps as quietly as my body. Thanks to Heaven, I find myself tranquil, and sleep more easily than when I was allowed by all to be a King.

#### JUXON.

I am thankful for your Majesty's good disposition.—You are prepared, Sire, to quit a world, which you have found so full of trouble.

#### KING.

I trust I am.—Colonel Tomlinson, I saw you not; excuse me.—You are well, I hope.

#### COLONEL.

My gracious Lord.

#### KING.

Juxon, if happier times for England
should

should arrive, 'ere you come to meet me in Heaven, do not forget to declare that the kindness of my keeper has greatly softened my prison cares.

#### JUXON.

My Lord, I shall remember.
(*Colonel Tomlinson bows.*)

#### KING.

Here comes my darling child—my gracious dear Elizabeth!—I dread her vehemence of grief!—My good Juxon, I will attend you in my chamber presently. Colonel, I have your leave to talk alone with my daughter?

#### COLONEL.

Most surely, Sire.
(*Juxon and Tomlinson go out.*)

*Enter* PRINCESS ELIZABETH.

#### KING.

Come, my child, and receive my blessing.

(*The*

(*The Princess kneels; the King raises and embraces her.*)

#### PRINCESS.

Alas!—how soon will that happiness be denied me!—Oh, Sir, is it then certain I have nothing more to hope?—Can it be possible these wicked men will dare to touch your sacred life?—It cannot be; there cannot exist such barbarity in human nature!

#### KING.

Alas, my child, too certainly, there can! — To-morrow, Elizabeth! — to-morrow, at this time!—Oh God, support her fortitude!

#### ELIZABETH.

What say you, Sir!—to-morrow!—Oh Heavens, have they then———

(*She leans against the King.*)

#### KING.

Recover, my dearest child.—Hear me, Elizabeth.—Ah, my God, thou seest my anguish

anguish—hear my prayer—sooth and console my child!

ELIZABETH, *(falling on her knees.)*
Hear me also, oh my God!—Save my father—spare him!—Oh, spare him, who taught me to know and to serve thee!

KING.
Rise, my child.—You rend my heart. If I die, it must be the will of Heaven. Heaven is pleased to make bad men its instruments, doubtless for some good cause.—If, by dying, I serve my country, I die contented.

ELIZABETH.
Oh, my murdered, martyred father.— Oh mother, my dear mother, where are you!

KING.
Elizabeth!—alas—there you touch the string of all my woes!—Thy mother, thy dear and virtuous mother, whom I have loved with undeviating tenderness,
what

what will she suffer when she hears of this!—For thee, Elizabeth, be composed, and hear the latest charge which I shall ever give thee.—Hear now my last advice; to-morrow I shall have much to do!—Attend to me, and let my blessing follow your observance of my words.

#### ELIZABETH.

So help me Heaven, as to the hour of my death I shall remember them!

#### KING.

If thou art happy enough again to see thy mother, bear to her my latest commendations; tell her that, in the moment of death, my soul shall thank and bless her, for her tenderness and truth.—Tell her I conjure her to forgive whatever errors in my conduct may have rendered her unhappy; and tell her that, as my soul hopes for eternal rest, *I have never, even in thought, departed from the love and truth*

*truth I owe her.*——Thou wilt remember this?

ELIZABETH.

Remember!

KING.

Bid her be comforted; and to thee, my child, I leave the charge of consolation; the tenderness of your sex will fit you for the office.—To your young sister I leave my love and blessing.—*Obey your mother in all things, except in the article of Religion; I charge you on my blessing never to forsake that in which you have been educated.*—To thy brothers, Charles and James, commend me also; tell them, above all earthly things, to seek the welfare of their country.—I have left other messages for them with my good Juxon; but charge them also, not to suffer the gaieties of a luxurious Court to dissipate those virtuous sentiments they have imbibed from me.

ELIZABETH.

ELIZABETH.

Oh, my Lord, my father, fear not your children ever can forget the glorious example you set before them.

KING.

And now, my child, embrace me.—(*They embrace, with tears.*) For the present, farewell.—My reverend friend waits for me.—I shall see thee again. Farewell, Elizabeth—farewell! (*He goes out.*)

ELIZABETH.

He will see me again!—But how soon will that dear blessing be denied me!—Murdered, basely murdered, in the prime of his years; after to-morrow I shall never see him more!—Oh, yes, in Heaven we shall meet, where I feel I soon shall join him. (*She goes out.*)

*Scene closes.*

**END OF THE FIRST PART.**

## PART THE SECOND.

---

JUXON. HERBERT.

**HERBERT.**

AH, my Lord, what a day is this!—Will the bloody sacrifice be compleated?

**JUXON.**

I fear it will!—Cromwell's heart, hardened by ambition, is inaccessible to pity or remorse; and no one else has power to save my Royal Master.—My aged heart shrinks within me!—My God, support me in this dreadful trial! Enable me to prepare my King to act with dignity this last sad scene, which closes all!

**HERBERT.**

My Lord, our Royal Master suffers less than we do.—He is calm, tranquil, even
unusually

unusually chearful.—Just now, he desired me to *employ more than usual pains in dressing and preparing him for so great a solemnity.* \*

### JUXON.

I almost dread to enquire for the unhappy Princess!

### HERBERT.

Alas! my Lord, notwithstanding her early years, she shews an extreme feeling for the misfortunes of her family; they have early taught her to reflect, and advanced her judgment beyond her years. She looks upon her father as something of a superior nature to human beings in general; and she deplores, with excessive anguish, his approaching death!—She has passed a sleepless night in tears and faintings.—Who comes here?

\* See Hume's History.

*Enter* FAIRFAX.

JUXON.

General Fairfax!—may I believe my sight?

FAIRFAX.

You may, my Lord.—It is that mistaken, duped, unhappy man!

JUXON.

I know your character too well, General, to believe you come to insult the misfortunes you have in so great a measure caused.—But, permit me to say, the short time my Royal Master has to live, ought to be left undisturbed by the presence of his cruel enemies.

FAIRFAX.

Ah, my Lord, I forgive you these sharp words, since you know not my heart.—I come not to insult or interrupt a dying man.—It is true, I have been the enemy of Charles Stuart.

JUXON.

JUXON.

My Lord!

FAIRFAX.

Expect not I will give him a title he has forfeited.—He is no longer King.—I wished to dethrone a man, whom from my heart I believe capable of a design to subvert and overturn our liberties.—But to this base and cruel murder, I am not a party.—I came hither, my Lord, to declare to you, and to request you will declare to Charles Stuart——

JUXON.

I know no such person.

FAIRFAX, *(smiling.)*

We will not dispute on that score.—Call him what you please.—But bear witness to him, that Fairfax, tho' the enemy of his tyranny, is not the enemy of his person, nor can endure the thought of expiating his errors with his blood.—I go to try my intereſt to ſave him, moſt ſincerely wiſhing it may avail.

#### JUXON.

There is ſuch a mixture in your diſcourſe, my Lord, that I know not what to think of it.

#### FAIRFAX.

Think of it as it appears, my heart is on my lips.—I go.—I will not ſtay any longer, leaſt I ſhould ſeem to inſult the fallen.

#### JUXON.

May God proſper your good intentions!

#### FAIRFAX.

Amen!—My Lord, I can boldly ſay, Amen to that prayer, ſince it includes all I deſire to obtain.   (*He goes out.*

### JUXON. HERBERT.

#### JUXON.

Herbert, what are we to think of this?

#### HERBERT.

HERBERT.

Fairfax is, I am sure, sincere.—He is too noble to dissemble.—Beside, to what end should he wish to deceive us?

JUXON.

I know not; but I dare not hope!

HERBERT.

Alas! my Lord, I fear indeed his interest cannot now avail.—Within sight of the scaffold, will Cromwell consent to lose his victim?—That which he has refused to the entreaties and menaces of all the Courts of Europe, will he grant to the prayers of Fairfax?

JUXON.

No—there is no hope!—But, at least, it is gratifying, to observe, how much all good people revolt at this murder!

HERBERT.

Fairfax is an instance how difficult it is to stop short, when once we have entered the paths of rebellion, or, as it is now called, reformation.—Could he, could many others, have foreseen this dreadful catastrophe, or known before-hand what deluges of blood would be poured forth in this cause, would they have dared to stir in it? May all future reformers consider, 'ere they begin so difficult a task, how it is likely to end.—Let them reflect, how much they will deplore their misguided zeal in removing slight errors, when they have lighted the flames of civil war!—What direful images present themselves, under that horrid name!—Father against son; brother against brother.—Every social virtue, every endearing tie, broken. The land desolate; arts destroyed.—Murder—rapine—and breach of faith, drawing down the vengeance of God on a guilty people!—Surely, the greatest blessings are dearly purchased, at such a rate!—How then can mistaken men bar-

ter

ter peace, and all the virtues which attend her, for the mere shadow of chimerical liberty, which cannot long be preserved?

JUXON.

You say true.—These hypocritical * *Levellers* affect not to consider, that if they destroy dignities, a short time must unavoidably exalt some men above others. Superior talents, excellent virtues, even exquisite art, will, by degrees, raise one man above another; and even if all men could be equal, should they wish to be so? Has not God evidently designed difference of station, that the rich might assist the poor, and the poor labour for the rich? But no more of this, we forget in these useless disquisitions our present wretched situation. Here comes the King.

* A set of people so called, as well in the time of Charles the First, as in our days.

*Enter*

*Enter the* KING, *and* COL. TOMLINSON.

#### KING.

My good Juxon, the sight of you rejoices my heart.—How pleasant it is to know, that, amid all my distresses, I have at least preserved a few sincere friends.

#### COLONEL.

Your Majesty may well preserve your friends, since your virtue makes friends of your enemies.

#### JUXON.

Fairfax has been here, Sire; he requests me to protest to your Majesty his abhorrence of the present measures, and his earnest endeavours to counteract them.

#### KING.

I am gratified by his wishes, but feel assured they will avail nothing.

#### JUXON.

Your Majesty has heard the noble effort
of

of your four friends, Richmond, Hertford, Southampton, and Lindesay? *

KING.

No, my good Juxon.

JUXON.

They have been with the Parliament; they have declared that all your Majesty's measures, which have displeased the Parliament, were advised by them; that, therefore, they alone were responsible for their effect; and concluded by desiring to die in your Majesty's stead; happy if by the price of their blood, they could purchase your safety!

KING.

Oh, generous men!—Heroes, whose names shall never be forgotten!—Could they believe I would accept such a sacrifice!—Could they think me so poor a wretch, to accept my life at such a price!

* See Hume.

JUXON.

#### JUXON.

Ah, Sire, could their offer have been accepted, they would not have permitted you to hesitate; but, alas! such a generous effort could avail only to mark their names for ever with glory!

#### KING.

Juxon, time draws on.—Let me speak awhile alone—before—before I taste the bitterness of death, in parting from my children.

(*Tomlinson and Herbert retire.*)

#### KING.

My worthy friend, while you spoke to me of those heroic men, with what a pang my heart has struck me!

#### JUXON.

Sire?

#### KING.

Have I deserved such firm, such steady friendship?—I, alas! who basely, and like a coward, signed the warrant for the execution

cution of the noble Strafford, when my whole soul revolted against the measure! I wanted firmness.—I dared not refuse to ratify an unjust sentence, and behold the retribution of Heaven, I perish by an unjust sentence myself!*

#### JUXON.

Your Majesty so feelingly bewails an action, which your real friends will not endeavour to excuse, that doubtless your repentance, in the sight of Heaven, will avail to expiate the error.

#### KING.

Error!—Give it a harsher name, good Juxon, nor palliate the crimes of a dying man.

#### JUXON.

Ah, Sire, how few like you can look back on a long life, and see but one action which wounds their conscience.—How

* See Hume.

few like you, so exposed to temptation, would thus deeply lament a fault arising from that weakness which some times overpowers the best of men.—Yet think not, in this awful hour, I dare to flatter. It was a crime; but a crime for which I dare hope and believe your deep repentance has long since obtained your pardon.

#### KING.

I thank you, my good friend, both for your manly freedom and kind comfort. I trust, in the infinite mercies of my Redeemer, both this and all my other crimes will be forgiven.

*Enter* TOMLINSON.

#### TOMLINSON.

My duty, Sire, obliges me to warn you the morning advances, and that the hour is near——

#### KING.

You say true, good Tomlinson—I had forgotten.

forgotten.———Oh! Juxon, not till this moment has my courage failed, nor is it now the near approach of death alarms me. I shrink not from the axe, but from the pangs, the anguish of my helpless children! Bid them come hither, I must over-rule this anguish!

JUXON, (*aside.*)
Fairfax comes not—there is no hope!

HERBERT.
Sire, the Princess, and the Duke of Gloucester, are here.

*Enter* PRINCESS ELIZABETH, *and the* DUKE.

ELIZABETH, (*running to throw herself at her father's feet.*)
Oh, my King and father, bless me— once more bless your wretched daughter!

KING.
God bless both my children!
(*He raises, and embraces them.*)

ELIZABETH.

ELIZABETH.

Ah, my father, ſtill, ſtill hold me in your arms!—Oh, my God, why muſt I be torn from them!—Why may I not die with my father, and finiſh my miſeries and my life together!

KING.

My child, many days are yet in ſtore for you; I will hope, happy ones.

ELIZABETH.

Happy!—for me!—What, my father, can you believe I ever ſhall forget this dreadful moment; theſe aweful, horrid preparations!—Can a child, who ſees her father bleed almoſt before her eyes, ever hope for happineſs again?—No, Sire, no; my whole ſoul devotes itſelf, from this terrible moment, to unmixed, though unavailing ſorrow!

GLOUCESTER.

Siſter, you make my father ſad; why do you?—Father, tell me what they are going to do with you?—What is that wooden place built up for?—Are they going to crown you, as I have heard Kings are crowned?

KING.*

Yes, my child—to crown me, as I hope, with a crown which shall endure for ever.

GLOUCESTER.

What *now?*

KING.

Yes.—" Now will they cut off thy father's head. (*He takes him on his knee; Gloucester looks at him stedfastly.*) Mark, child, what I say; they will cut off my head, and perhaps make thee a King; but mark what I say, thou must not be a King, so long as thy brothers, Charles and James, are alive.—They will cut off thy brothers heads, when they can get them into their power; and thy head too

* For this speech, and Gloucester's answer, see Hume.

they will cut off, at laſt; therefore, I charge thee, do not be made a King by them."

GLOUCESTER, (*with a deep ſigh.*)
" I will be torn in pieces firſt!"

KING, (*embracing him with tears.*)
Oh, my God, I thank thee for giving ſuch determined virtue to this infant!—Glouceſter, my dear Glouceſter, thou wilt not forget thy father!—Look at me, my child; take notice of this grey head, from which my enemies have torn the crown;* and tell me, thou wilt remember me?

GLOUCESTER.
Oh yes, indeed, indeed; and when I ſee mama, ſhall I tell her not to grieve?

KING.
Yes, Glouceſter; yes, my child!—

† Charles the Firſt uſes the expreſſion of " this grey diſcrowned head," in a copy of verſes written during his impriſonment.

Juxon,

Juxon, would one not think this infant read my heart, and wifhed to footh its deepeft care?

KING, (*fetting down the child.*)

Farewell, Gloucefter; farewell, my child; God blefs thee!

GLOUCESTER.

Oh, father—don't leave us!—Let us go with you; indeed we fhould chufe it!

KING, (*ftruggling with his emotion.*)

You will come to me.

GLOUCESTER.

Let us go now, father.—I fhall be afraid, when you are gone; for the foldiers frown fo, I think they will hurt me, only I know you won't let them; but when you are gone, there will be nobody to take care of us.

### KING.

He rends my heart!——Elizabeth, my girl, what quite overcome.—Come hither, and embrace me!—(*a pauſe.*)—Once more—Oh! once more.—How trembling nature lingers!

### ELIZABETH, (*embracing the King.*)

Oh, my father, I feel, I feel, I ſhall ſoon follow you—but while I live, as the beſt means of proving my love and my affliction, believe I will do nothing unworthy of your child.

### KING.

I thank you, for this promiſe.—You have already my inſtructions.—Talk of me ſometimes to Glouceſter; is it weakneſs to wiſh he may remember an unfortunate father?—Farewell, fa—farewell!——Now all is over, and I can meet death

death without another pang!—Thy mother, Elizabeth, thy mother—remember all I have said to thee!—Farewell!

(*The King, Juxon, Herbert, and Tomlinson go out.—The Princess faints in the arms of her women, and the Scene closes.*)

☞ For the Sequel of this affecting Story, as well as for several Passages, the Reader is referred to Hume's History of England.

END OF THE SECOND VOLUME.

www.ingramcontent.com/pod-product-compliance
Lightning Source LLC
LaVergne TN
LVHW061214060426
835507LV00016B/1934